This book belonged to CONSORD OSBORNE before 1991

W9-CTZ-952

Beyond The Bath

A DREAMER'S GUIDE

Thomas Cowan

A QUARTO BOOK

RUNNING PRESS
BOOK PUBLISHERS
PHILADELPHIA, PENNSYLVANIA

This book belonged to CONSORD OSBORNE before 1991

A QUARTO BOOK

Copyright © 1983 by Quarto Marketing Ltd.
All rights reserved under the Pan-American and International
Copyright Conventions. No part of this publication may be
reproduced, stored in a retrieval system, or transmitted,
in any form or by any means, electronic, mechanical,
photocopying, recording, or otherwise, without the prior
written permission of the copyright owner.

9 8 7 6 5 4 3 2 1
Digit on the right indicates the number of this printing.

Library of Congress Cataloging in Publication Number
83--061775

ISBN 0-89471-225-X (cloth)
ISBN 0-89471-223-3 (paperback)
ISBN 0-89471-224-1 (library binding)

BEYOND THE BATH was produced and prepared by
Quarto Marketing Ltd.
32-33 Kingly Court, London W1, England

Editor: Gene Santoro
Art Director: Richard Boddy
Designer: Abby Kagan

Typeset by BPE Graphics, Inc.
Color separations by Hong Kong Scanner Craft Company Ltd.
Printed and bound in Hong Kong by Leefung-Asco Printers Ltd.

This book may be ordered from the publisher.
Please include $1.00 postage.
But try your bookstore first.

Running Press Book Publishers
125 South 22nd Street
Philadelphia, Pennsylvania 19103

ABOUT THE AUTHOR

Thomas Cowan is a widely published author with a special involvement in home and personal improvement. Among his previous books are *Great Kids Rooms, The Home Security Guide, How to Remove Spots and Stains,* and *Free Things for Home-owners.* His poetry has been published in *Spoon River Quarterly* and *Origins,* among other periodicals. In addition, he is on the editorial board of the *Dream Network Bulletin,* where his column "Dreamwatch" appears regularly.

Contents

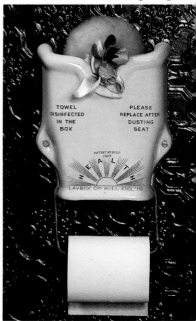

This Japanese-style bathroom successfully combines many unexpected textures. The natural brick of the curved ceiling; the clean white parchment shades that partially cover the window; the silver-plated brick inset on the end wall; the smooth blond wood that trims the tub and matches the bamboo hamper; the tight, foamy carpet that adds a soft area around the tub. Cotton, wood, paper, and brick all interweave simply and neatly—a perfect setting for the deep green plants and the two slender candle stands. As in a Japanese garden, the seemingly "empty" spaces between these materials are as full and textured as the walls and floors and ceiling themselves.

Introduction

*T*he door closes behind you, and you find that you have entered a world of seclusion and intimacy, a realm where the very private suggests the very secret, a place where you can be yourself. No matter where the bathroom is located, no matter the size, color, or decor, when you ease the door shut and turn on the light, the room is yours. And for the next few minutes or hours, your needs and desires activate this unique space, bring it to life, and give it purpose. Perhaps this intuitive sense of possession is what makes bathrooms such very personal spaces. For however long we linger within this sequestered environment, the rest of the world can be forgotten, outside pressures fade, each of us is once again both center and circumference of our lives. It is your time, your room, your invitation just to relax and refresh your body and spirit with rituals that cleanse, groom, renew.

When you step into the modern bathroom, you step into a space that can literally take you beyond the traditional bath. Materials developed in recent years provide tactile and visual experiences never dreamed of by preceding generations. Even though the fundamentals remain the same, new shapes, colors, textures, and arrangements have been incorporated into today's bathroom, changing its look and feeling dramatically. Not only in the fundamentals and permanent fixtures have there been design breakthroughs, but bathrooms now have startling new acquisitions that elicit the amazed inquiry, "What is *that* doing in the bathroom?" Indeed, the bathroom is being used for many more activities than the customary ones, rituals that pamper and nurture our bodies and spirits and treat ourselves—and our fantasies—in a holistic way.

Decorative touches for the bath can cater to your deepest needs or most fleeting whimsies. The objects, colors, patterns, and materials that yesterday would have been considered too bold or daring for the bathroom are finding their way into the world of tiles, taps, and towels. In fact, there no longer is a real distinction between what is appropriate in bathroom decoration and what is not. As the bathroom is increasingly designed for needs that go beyond the corporal, so are the flourishes that elevate the bathroom from utilitarian status to the level of high aesthetic and spiritual dimensions. When a room is created for personal comfort, pleasure, and self-expression, there should be few barriers between imagination and reality.

As we explore the world beyond the bath we encounter unusual spaces, areas that are clearly designed for bathing needs and yet somehow so ingeniously composed we not only applaud their uniqueness but find ourselves tarrying within them, exploring them, allowing them to work their subtle magic upon us. Some unusual bathrooms pop up in unexpected places; others so brilliantly utilize or adapt available space they seem the work of masters of illusion, suggesting by their arrangements that there is more here than meets the eye—indeed, more than meets even the unprepared imagination. In addition, some of the most unusual bathrooms split or join spaces, diverting some bathroom activities into their own private areas, or introducing them to other rooms and areas of the home: a sunken tub in the bedroom, a shower in the playroom.

Like other rooms, the bath has undergone a revolution in style. At one time a room either devoid of style or suggesting a style so bland it was hardly noticeable or worth comment, today's bath has been designed to go beyond the old frontiers as designers discover a virtual bazaar of exotic and stimulating styles. Introducing established styles from the past, inventing new variations on old themes, encouraging modes that defy accepted patterns so that you can express your own standards of taste, the modern bathroom designer, professional or amateur, is accomodating individual desires, whether conventional or eccentric.

Throughout the following pages, you will step into many bathrooms. Some may please you more than others, but our selection should stimulate you so that your own understanding of the bath will be revolutionized. For too long the bathroom has been a forgotten room, a neglected room. New attitudes toward the body and its relationship with the spirit have changed that attitude: a new understanding of health and pleasure has emerged and influenced the bath's design and uses. The rooms in the chapters that follow reflect that new consciousness, a consciousness that recognizes that the total human being possesses needs and desires that lead beyond the bath.

Fundamentals

In this spacious bathroom, the Zeta marble tiles on the walls, floors, and reflected in the mirrored ceiling enclose the bather in an environment of elegance and majesty. This study in variegated grays extends to include the large double tub, toilet, and bidet so that these major fixtures do not interrupt the dominant color theme. In fact, the latter two are carefully concealed behind the basin cabinets so that on entering this room, the eye traverses the room as a whole, not pausing over any one feature. Even the large double tub does not disrupt the overall statement. The mirrored cabinets below the sink reflect and intensify the deep striations suggestive of smooth marble stonework from which this entire room seems to be sculpted.

When the rites of hygiene that our ancestors performed outdoors were moved inside the house, it was called "progress"—a major advance in human evolution. We built a small, cramped chamber with floor, ceiling, and walls, and named it a "water closet." And it was little more than that: a closet with running water. Later the WC became an entire room—the bathroom. Today it still has the essentials of any room: floor, ceiling, walls. It requires light and ventilation. It needs a sense of style and a theme. We expect it to be pleasing.

But more than any other room in the house, the bath has trapped our imaginations into the tight definitions of the past; this prevents us from seeing "beyond the bath."

*T*ake windows, for example. They allow in light and fresh air, as they should. But they have been frosted, blinded, shaded, curtained, and shuttered in our desire to disappoint nosy neighbors. We want our privacy. And yet the many grooming and bathing activities we use the room for can benefit from the bright, honest light of the sun. A wide, vaulted skylight will satisfy our need for both intense light and privacy. But some bathroom windows defy convention. They boldly dare to be as long as the wall itself and open onto vistas that cascade down hillsides and race across valleys to distant mountains. More timid views peep out into private gardens of thick shrubs and dense foliage. But whether its view is of a sweeping landscape or the quiet contemplation of a private garden, the bathroom window means more than light and air, just as the bathroom itself has come to mean more than a "room with bath." It has become a place of refuge, a peaceful place that uncovers a deeper meaning

for the word "privacy." It is the privacy of spirit, as much as a privacy for the body. Even amid the pulsating beat of the city, a bathroom window high above the rush and clamor of traffic allows you to watch and reflect unseen—a vantage point where you are the unobserved observer.

Some bathrooms without the natural light of windows await your presence like perpetual evenings, their dim, dusky glow creating an aura of rest and relaxation reminiscent of twilight. You step in, and at your fingertips, at any time of day or night, is the power to create a world of light to match your mood. You flood the room with even light for activities that require clarity and discernment. Or you surround your image in the mirror with a soft yellow glow that sets you apart from the glare of the exterior world. However the bathroom admits or creates light, that light is special, for in it you are both the seer and the seen.

As bathrooms become increasingly stylish and thought-out in their designs and their functions, unconventional color combinations and striking patterns play a more prominent role in changing the whole "feel" of the bath. What would seem too busy for a bedroom or too lifeless for a living room can sound just the right note in a bathroom. Wallpaper emblazoned with large floral arrangements. A ceiling sprayed with psychedelic colors that seem to vibrate above you. Or a quiet monotone accented by a few simple objects.

*B*athroom walls can enclose many types of spaces: nooks, crannies, corners, as well as grand entrances, spacious exercise areas, and luxurious lounging quarters. Walls that shield the particular needs of you and your family. A large master bathroom can con-

This richly appointed room swoops upward to the center of a ceiling draped in the soft folds one would expect to find in an extravagant tent of an Oriental pasha. Notice how the centrifugal spokes of the floor-design mirror the billowed convolutions above, but in sharp radial lines, rather than the gentle wreaths that gird the ceiling. A room of square panels, hard rectangular shapes, and regal austerity, the ceiling and floor "circle" these squares and create an atmosphere that draws one's attention outward to the minor details on the periphery, such as the shallow gold chalices on the parchment-textured wall panels and golden goose heads on the Empire chair.

sist of several rooms, including an adjacent walk-in wardrobe, a powder room, "his and her" areas large enough to accommodate both grooming and dressing needs. Interesting effects can be achieved by the use of half-walls and movable partitions that turn corners into cloistered nooks where you store and use personal items.

The bathroom, particularly if not constructed in the traditional cube, allows your imagination to work a miniature marvel of intriguing color and design. A three-section folding screen isolates the commode area from the washbasin and mirror. A sliding door creates a separate room for the shower and tub. A sloped ceiling, too low for most activities, is just right over a tub; indeed, it becomes a canopy, suggesting coziness and protection.

*B*y its use of materials and colors, a bathroom can suggest other times, other places. Even the most modern can evoke an earlier, quieter era. Indeed, here is a world as primal as the elements themselves: water, heat, air, light, and the many manifestations of earth—tile, marble, fiber, porcelain, wood, metal, and stone itself. The

This study in red, white, and black demonstrates how easily a room of limited color range can express energy and vitality. Often rooms of only one or two colors have a static, frozen appearance that suggests lifelessness and lack of human warmth. But the human element is playfully alive and well in this bathroom, dancing up and down the walls in bright, frisky dots. The two mirrors over the basins catch the dots and spin them around even more, in trajectories that turn unexpected corners. The striped throw rug in front of the basins is a wise choice to continue the geometric movement but in strong parallel lines, a nice contrast to the zigzagging dots.

The collector's bathroom par excellence! A room for the creatively indecisive who enjoy finding and adding new items to their environment. On this wall-sized corkboard that extends the length of the tub are butterflies, mandalas, needlepoint, a lone bamboo fan, other odds and ends—all find a place of honor. Here is a wall material that is soft and warm, interestingly textured, and an obedient display board, ready, almost eager for new treasures, recently acquired doodads, or hand-scribbled reminders of things to do. With a wall of cork, your bathroom's decor can be varied by season, mood, or occasion. It can be as precious or as commonplace, as important or as trivial, as the many human moods that come with you each time you sink into this tub.

The surreal design that greets a bather in this tub is an optical illusion that can keep the mind guessing for hours about what tricks the eye is playing. The hand-painted custom-glazed tiles were especially prepared for the rear wall. Banners of black-and-white checkerboard pattern undulate and seem to blow in the wind. A caravan of gold camels marches serenely through the disarray of space and counterspace, a dreamlike image that stays in the memory as the dreamer wakes too quickly and the dream content fades forever.

A crazy-quilt effect can be achieved by mixing and matching tiles of various patterns and designs. Although the overall arrangement looks haphazard, a keen eye selected these tiles for color and tone. Each tile has a different geometric pattern fired upon it, but a muted earth tone runs through each, giving the walls around the tub a coherent look. No bright primary colors intrude. Even the stained-glass window with its sky view of birds and dragonflies on the wing continues the understated mood of a relaxing bath in an environment of soft earth textures. Notice how the small wooden tub and the starfish on the windowsill seem right at home—this is almost a natural habitat for wood and marine life.

most elemental needs can be satisfied in a setting as pure and basic as the elements of the enduring earth, surrounded by comforting earth tones.

Still, many of us have transformed the bath to match our high-tech world. The sleek, antiseptic bathroom provides a space-age world of gleaming utility, where not an inch is wasted. For today's fast-paced living, we can create an efficient room, where speed, utility, and a minimum of effort accomplish the primitive tasks over which our forebears lingered. We can step into a room devoid of frills, pared down from the fancy to the basic, where hygiene and easy-to-care-for materials meet in comfort and safety: plastic and polyurethane, aluminum and polyesters as jaunty as a rainbow, or the subdued glitter of steel and chrome in industrial design.

*A*s you peruse this chapter, you will discover bathroom fundamentals of many shapes, sizes, and styles, suggesting many moods: whimsical, practical, sensual, peaceful, startling, traditional, seductive, masculine, feminine—and some designs that defy all preconceived notions! Yes, because the private spaces of the bathroom are *your* spaces, they should be designed for your own personal enjoyment and self-expression. Of all the rooms in the house, the bathroom is unique, in that it is exceptionally personal and private, yet it is visited by most of your guests, some of whom may never peek into your bedroom or private study. It is a room that demands self-expression and self-indulgence because it invites you, your family, your friends, your lovers, to be self-indulgent—to relax, to be at ease, and to attend to the personal requirements of the body as well as the dreams and fantasies that renew the spirit.

This room showcases a striking use of
materials and color. The shag carpet leaves
the deep-burgundy geometry on the floor as
it gently curls up to cover the side of the tub.
Painted tiles enclose the tub area itself, but
the rest of the walls are left a smooth plaster
of twilight gray. By elevating the towel racks
to the height seen here, the designers have
continued the soft texture of the floor to eye
level, where fluffy red towels become, in
effect, wall hangings to break up the
dominant gray color. The bright plastic
fixtures of red and white introduce yet
another material to this room.

Up, up, and away! This brightly lighted
bath seems to float on air, high in a
rarefied atmosphere far removed from
corporal needs. In fact, a bather here could
almost think he or she was out of the body,
floating like these stylized clouds through a
Delft blue heaven. Even the heavy
fixtures—tub, toilet, bidet, and double
basin—have a billowy delicacy that seems to
defy gravity. They too look as weightless and
capable of flight as any lighter-than-air
machine. The tiles in this bathroom create
an ethereal effect in color, pattern, and
design, lulling even the weariest bather into
reveries that soar far above the mundane
problems of daily life.

Does this bathroom remind you of silk and satin? It should. The
acrylic materials used on the major fixtures are "white satin," a
creation of Twyfords Bathrooms, Stokes-on-Trent, England. The color
is ivory white but the feel is of satin, a finish that approximates the
texture of polished marble. The tiles are a silky white with a luxurious
soft sheen that absorbs light rather than reflects it harshly. In fact, the
silky, satinlike quality of this entire room reduces glare, unlike so
many bathrooms furnished with hard-surfaced materials that produce
glare spots and the "hot" coldness that disturbs. The strategically
located plants and painted tile provide appropriate finishing touches.

The fundamental colors of nature—brown, green, and blue—are represented here in this bathroom that very simply unites wood, leaf, and stone. The two windows, where one could have been built, lead the eye up and outward in a way that one large window would never do. The leafy glade outside and the natural light become more precious in this room when one realizes that the wall has been preserved as wall for privacy. The blue and blue-green mesh of tiles along the basin counter marries sky and water while complementing the blue toilet bowl. The unadorned touches of wood along the door, window frames, and toilet seat give this room a wonderfully wholesome and healthy feeling.

When this large room was converted into a bathroom, the designer chose to conceal the shower stall completely so that the old-fashioned tub (not shown here) would be the central focus. The shower was constructed in a spacious corner of the room, and the enclosure, including the door, was papered with Chinese panels to match the walls in the rest of the room. The leafy floral sanctuary for cardinals, bluebirds, and robins distracts the attention from the actual purpose of the area. But a discerning eye will spot the door's outline, the light switch, the raised base housing the floor tray to catch the runoff water. Unlike other bathrooms that frankly expose all the fixtures, this one judiciously chooses those that will enhance the overall design of the room and camouflages others, such as the shower, that would detract.

This simple tub incorporates features not often found in one bathroom. Raised, this peninsular fixture extends into the middle of the room from one wall, has an island quality created by the surrounding light from the two French windows on either side. It also has the depth of a hot tub for total submerging. In fact, entering this tub requires agility. The high sides and raised dais give it an imposing quality, an aura of prominence it deserves in a room so spare that the tub and the pleasures of bathing become the primary theme.

Flooded by light from this circular skylight, this bathroom demonstrates how a few color variations and a plenitude of light can enrich a basically colorless room. Varying shades of green from the hanging ferns and the array of magentas and lavenders highlight the luxurious marbled tiles and clean, uncluttered walls. The larger areas of color in the hanging plants and towels are echoed in miniature by small flowering plants that balance opposite corners of the tub. Even without the full mirror, this bathroom would be an oasis of light and space, but with it, the room is a true celebration of openness and radiance.

This country bathroom with a small shower and tub unit looks as if it were carved right out of the earth itself. The exposed brick wall and floor, the earth tone shower tiles, the pine trim, and the spectacular burst of plant life and sunlight give this room the warm, comfortable atmosphere that looks as relaxing and isolated as a hidden forest glen.

The foliage and hanging baskets outside seem to be interior decorations. The wooden door has a panel of smoked, mottled glass that catches the light and color so that they, more than the glass itself, provide privacy.

This triptych screen of beveled glass in dark rich wood is a partition that does not partition, a divider that does not divide. Totally transparent, this folding screen separates the bathroom area of the room only in the bather's mind, a psychic scrim that allows the room to wend on past the bureau into the bath and beyond. Dark splash tiles over the tub match the wooden frame, creating a bathing area that in spite of its open vulnerability is self-contained and protected. An ideal way to define space by function without constructing barriers that fragment space into smaller segments.

This room is designed to create two distinct areas: a recess to accommodate the primary bathroom fixtures of tub, toilet, and basin, and a more immediate space that leads off from the bedroom bordered by the dresser and the folding screen. And yet these two spaces fit together and embrace each other by the use of color and furnishings. For example, the dressing table beneath the window, if not painted white, would be a companion piece to the mahogany dresser, but instead becomes part of the white ensemble of tub and toilet. The throw rug at the far end has the same coloring as the standing screen in the foreground.

The beauty of this bathroom is not to be concealed behind the traditional solid door that signifies privacy and isolation. Rather, this interior is so richly decorated with the luminous power of the orange and sand-colored obelisks, the bright yellow flowers, and the vibrating pattern of the blond cabinetry that to shut it off from view would waste the potential here for a dramatic and luxurious moment even for someone just passing by. The door, therefore, is not solid but contains four cross-hatched glass panels. The screenlike effect makes the bathroom seem more a part of the house, while still maintaining its separateness.

The door that graces this sunroom is an exquisite example of leaded, beveled glasswork. Hearts, diamonds, and teardrops interlace in a magnificent grille that is the perfect foil for the strong, steady lines and grains of wood that dominate this room. Generous amounts of sunlight can enter this hot-tub environment, allowing it to double as a solarium for flowering plants. Even when not in use (as shown here), with the tub covered, the stairs used as pedestals for potted plants, the room exudes an eye-catching energy. Lovely to look at, delightful to use, it is an unpretentious triumph of sunlight, glass, and wood.

Bathing is as much a recreational activity as it is a hygienic ritual and can be enjoyed in the natural surroundings of open air, fresh light, and rich summer foliage. A whirlpool such as this one is a welcome sight for guests arriving for brunch on warm sunny days. Generous skylights let out the steamy air that in small, completely enclosed rooms grows stale and hard to breathe, thus preventing the room from serving other purposes such as dining. The smooth flagstone floor is cool on bare feet and easy to sponge up when wet. This airy room of stone and rough-hewn beams is a perfect transition between the interior of the home and the spacious lawn outside.

Enhanced by the surrounding lush greenery, a long soak in this corner tub is as restful and healthy as a bath in a natural spring lost in a quiet forest. Vertical blinds can be closed for total privacy or left partially open for enjoying the view. A gentle breeze from the ceiling fan will keep the air stirring and prevent the choked-up atmosphere so typical of many bathrooms. On balmy days the windows can be opened to let in fresh air, and riding the stationary bike will be as healthful and pleasant as a tour through the countryside. Here is a room to stimulate the senses with nature's bountiful pleasures.

Surrounding the tub with a gracefully curved wall of glass brick creates a prismatic effect that brings color and light into an otherwise stark bathing area. Desiring a basically empty space, the designer of this bathroom has achieved a feeling of enclosure that is still remarkably open and spacious; bathers here will enjoy a privacy that is not claustrophobic, guarded by a wall that protects and separates without barring the outside world of color, movement, and light. Solid yet delicate, this glass brick wall suggests the beauty of crystal, an element that is hard, durable, and yet constantly changing as the light breaks through it.

Another example of glass brick, this time separating the shower area from the rest of the bathroom. Curved to complete the circular shape that rounds off this room, the brick partition is a permanent shower "curtain" that lets in light from the outer area, thus solving the problem of how to illuminate the shower cubicle without installing additional lighting fixtures. Notice how the faucets for the shower, located outside the actual shower, let you adjust the water temperature before entering—a necessity since this glass brick "curtain" cannot be pulled partially back while you turn on the water and get the temperature just right. A substantial, single-unit towel rack and grab bar ingeniously runs the entire length of the wall, from below the mirror into the shower.

2

Permanent Fixtures

Here is a bathroom with space to spare, and the free-standing tub and glass enclosed shower stall hold the commanding position in the center of this capacious room. The far corners are united by precise red tiles, set off by two concentric blue borders. The room's seeming spareness does not detract from the ceremonial atmosphere, which centers on the bath-shower ensemble where bathers can luxuriate in imperial fantasies—treatment that invites one to be the focus of attention. Even the two mirror-plated basins stand in respectful attendance, waiting to perform their duties. Who could shower in such a spotlight and not indulge the secret exhibitionism that resides in our celebrity daydreams?

The bathroom is primarily a world of running water, an environment designed to accommodate steam, moisture, humidity, dampness. The bathroom's major fixtures are the permanent receptacles to control this constant flow and use of water. Whether for a total cleansing in a shower, spot bathing at the basin when you are rushed, or a complete submerging of the body in a deep tub full of scented water—the tub, the basin, the shower, as well as the toilet and bidet, are the essentials of most bathrooms.

*T*here are two kinds of people in the world: those who shower and those who bathe. We all know people who proudly claim they "never take a bath" and wax eloquent about the more hygienic and stimulating virtues of the shower. The "shower people" seem to have morality on their side, as they smugly disavow the decadent self-indulgence that seems to be the *raison d'etre* of a bath, especially when enhanced with bubbles, oils, or perfumes. And the "bath people" admit they emerge less clean, although feeling good. The old Puritan prejudice against wasting anything is now an ecological concern for saving water. Caught up in the modern mania for speed and efficiency, we find it harder to defend the bath. Indeed, it is sometimes even hard to *find* a bath nowadays. Accelerated lifestyles frequently leave no time—or room—for the long, lazy bath, which even some of the more militant shower addicts will admit to indulging in occasionally. For deep down, we are all "closet bathers."

And yet if you can defy the moralists, you will discover that never before has bathing been as wonderfully luxuriant as it can now be. The art and science of tub design has married the newest materials with some of the old-est fantasies. The cold, slippery porcelain baths of yesteryear can be replaced with warmer and softer materials such as teakwood (treated with up-to-date finishes to prevent leakage and bacteria buildup) or the many types of plastic that permit unusual contours and color combinations. Always in style is the ageless majesty of marble. And the shapes and placement: a compressed tub neatly wedged into a corner, an island tub designed for two, a peninsular tub stretching out into the room. Some baths are raised up on a dais; others are sunken into the floor. While the tub should fit the room in both size and design, its inner contour is meant to fit you. When properly sculpted, the contour should position the body comfortably while lounging. No-slip areas on the bottom and grab rails provide safety. Extra-wide aprons and handy service ledges let you set bottles, soaps, and brushes nearby—or a book and a sandwich, or perhaps a candle and a glass of wine for a romantic tryst.

*H*ardly a trip to the bathroom does not utilize the wash basin. As if it were a sacred shrine, we always go up to it, whether for a cold splash of water on the face, for washing hands, or for a simple drink. Even when not used, the basin holds our most frequently used toilet articles for easy access or supports us as we lean forward to gaze closely into the mirror. Like the tub, the bathroom sink comes in a variety of styles: the traditional wall-hung sink preferred by many because it can be adjusted to any height; the inset sink, recessed into the wall itself; the pedestal basin that stands out from the wall conceals the plumbing in its stem; and the useful cabinet-top basin with a wide counter for toilet accessories and storage space underneath. Your basin may be shell-shaped, oval, round, or square, and decorated with your favorite colors and patterns, or it might even be a double sink to accommodate you and another during the bathroom rush hours in the morning and evening.

The fixtures for a tub or basin can provide character or amusement. Stately brass, chrome- or gold-plated, colorful enamel, mother-of-pearl—taps come in assorted shapes, including the reliable cross-headed and gear-shaped knobs that are easy to grasp with soapy fingers. Recent innovations include levers that lift, twist, or pull, some combining both hot and cold spigots in one fixture. You may want to splurge, let your sense of fantasy run wild, with taps resembling friendly water creatures such as dolphins, swans, ducks, or the puckish faces of naiads, mermaids, and tritons. For the ecologically minded, a spout with a spray head will save water, although it takes longer to fill the bowl. And to wash your hair easily in the basin when a full shower is not necessary, a stylish pillar spout lifts the water high enough to duck your head beneath.

*T*he one permanent fixture of the modern bath that has improved over the centuries only in aesthetics and hygiene is the toilet. It is still a functional anomaly today, for it does not adequately meet the biological need for which it was invented. The most natural position for elimination is the low squat, in which the thighs gently press against the abdomen, not an upright sitting position at almost chair level. As if nature will not be foiled even by our foibles, we spontaneously lean forward and cross our arms over our thighs to approximate the more satisfying posture. Some toilets incorporate footrests on either side to allow

Here's an unusual shower, a grottolike cocoon that makes washing fun and easy. The brick exterior has a sturdy bake-oven look, nestled unobtrusively in the corner of the room made from the same bland brick. But step inside, and you enter a kaleidescopic world of colorful mosaic and patchwork fantasy. A porthole window allows the daylight to enter, and a light recessed behind the arched entrance illuminates this cozy space at night. A perfect way to turn an unused corner into a shower with traditional materials, a shower that is not only as functional as the newer plastic ones, but that serves as a conversation piece as well.

the body to bend even farther forward into a surrogate squat. But for all its disadvantages, the modern toilet is a definite improvement over the old low chamber pot in terms of convenience and sanitary requirements.

In our efforts to conceal the toilet, either out of embarrassment or a narrow sense of propriety and aesthetics, some toilets have been boxed in or sunken into tiled or wooden ledges. Or we have hidden them in a *chaise percee*—an elaborate, throne like chair intended to pass itself off as an expensive or merely quaint piece of furniture. While achieving the goal of hiding the toilet, these designs offer no legroom at all, forcing us into an even more upright sitting position.

Still, the toilet signifies a universal concern for cleanliness. For when it comes to toilets, the most sanitary is surely the most appealing. Here is one case where indeed truth determines beauty, and beauty truth.

The bidet, French for old nag, is a rarity in the English-speaking world. One wonders, considering the pride we take in the virtue of cleanliness, why the bidet has not yet become a common feature of American and British bathrooms. For the Calvinist, cleanliness really is next to godliness, and the bidet may still recall of the decadence and immorality often associated with Continental Europe. In some minds, then, the bidet will always remain primarily an elaborate and awfully conspicuous method of contraception. But, in truth, the bidet's warm spray of water affords a more sanitary and satisfying way of cleansing oneself than the dry-paper method.

*T*he *coup de grace* of any bathroom is a steambath, sauna, or whirlpool. Once considered luxurious and exotic ways to cleanse the body, these bathing ensembles are now available in kit form and are becoming ever more popular as we discover their value in a holistic approach to health. Indeed, when you experience their total effect, you realize that the mind and spirit also have need of cleansing and revitalization. Steam and the heat of the sauna open the pores and allow trapped impurities to escape. In the process, the steambath stimulates circulation, and the sauna loosens and relaxes tense muscles. In each, your breathing deepens as you inhale the hot air condensed with steam or desiccated by the moisture-absorbing wood of the sauna. A fragrant touch of eucalyptus or birch enhances the otherworldly atmosphere and carries you to Greece, Rome, or Scandinavia. When finished, step beneath a cold shower, if snow or an icy fjord is not handy, and you're ready to face the world again. Or quietly rinse off in a warm shower; then drift off to bed and sleep.

The hydrotherapy of the whirlpool can reinvigorate you even on the most tiresome day. Strategically placed jet streams of aerated water massage your body like strong, gentle fingers. The mantralike bubbling and gurgling is reassuring and mesmerizing while your body and mind relax into peace and contemplation. In recent years, the whirlpool concept has become more sociable with the invention of the hot tub, a large, often wooden tub of aerated water that can comfortably hold you and several friends or an entire family. You don't have to live in sunny California, where they were first introduced, to enjoy a hot tub—indoor models are rapidly becoming part of the bathing scene everywhere.

This magnificent Victorian setting for the bathroom basin is a masterpiece in itself. Exquisitely carved oak, tiered and paneled with mirrors, offers a variety of shelf, counter, and cabinet spaces. While large and massive, taking up most of the wall, this handsomely carved chiffonier appears lighter that it is because of the structural openness created by its many mirrors. The dark-green plants are spontaneous decorative touches for the natural wood grains that present such an appealing background for the foliage. Like other bathroom settings, this one clearly and boldly displays the broad-lipped white porcelain basin itself.

This oddly angled tub enclosed in brown tiles has a canister overhead that releases a miniature rain shower. One might wonder how the spray from this shower, bouncing off bare shoulders and head, can be controlled without a shower curtain or doors for protection. But on closer look, we see that this unique shower is an unusual, whimsical method for filling the tub. More serious cleansing is done with the hand-held shower head attached to the wall. A large, inviting area, this tub and shower caters to the playfulness in us that enjoys sitting beneath a waterfall or running outdoors in a summer shower to sit in the grass.

In addition to sunken bathtubs there are also sunken bathrooms. This one, just three steps down from the outdoors, has an earth-tiled floor that complements the stonework around the large window. In this sparsely decorated room every detail is chosen to emphasize the tub—a blue-black exterior with brass feet and matching fixtures that contrast sharply with its pure-white porcelain interior. The wall tiles, a delicate pattern of deep-blue geometry against a white field, capture the same color mood as the tub. Other trimmings of royal blue complete this subterranean setting—a comfortable, stylish room dug into the earth with a window high above the tub for light and air and a rough stone wall that suggests a special space where a bather renews contact with nature and re-establishes a special place within it.

Possibly the most advanced style of bathing equipment available is seen here in this multileveled bath from Teuco, contoured to fit either the reclining or sitting body for long periods of time. Here is a bath that eliminates the stress and numbness of muscles that often occur while soaking, and which defeats one of the bath's primary purposes: the pure pleasure of relaxation. In this model, you lie against the slanted backrest; the no-slip texture on the bottom keeps you securely in place. Armrests prevent the shoulder strain that comes from holding a book or newspaper. Controls conveniently located on the side eliminate the necessity of squirming to the far end to add more hot water. For a more stimulating bath, this tub easily converts to whirlpool and also offers a hand-held shower head.

A sunken tub that reflects the owner's hardy athleticism. Spare, lean, masculine, this bathing chamber goes back to the basics of good health—exercise, hygiene, relaxation—in surroundings that inspire health care. The earth-stone floor descends quickly into the bathing area. The few simple furnishings do not distract the mind from the strongly stated purpose of the room. The French doors at the end stand as silent reminders that the ultimate goal of this room is to lead outward from a pool of earthlit waters into the invigorating, sunlit day. A bathing area that in spite of its permanency seems transient—a momentary pause in a life of rigorous activity.

This multipurpose room contains both lounge area and bath—a real retreat from the hectic pressures of the day. The satisfying color combination—tans and blue—pervades the entire room. The mottled tiles wander all over the room, thus creating a tiered architectural effect of a monument whose massive bulk rests solidly on tightly woven carpet. Both carpet and tile have an iridescent quality, which selective lighting transforms into the bright-dark splotchy effect of an underwater setting. A truly masculine chamber, secure, solid, comforting—as far removed from the world as a private, subterranean cavern hidden at the bottom of the sea.

This gold-plated basin from Consulat utilizes a steel faucet that produces a sleek sheet of water as it fills the bowl. The Niagara effect, shimmeringly beautiful, matches the luxurious surfaces that surround it. This translucent film of falling water catches the steel and gold tones of the basin and reflects them with an almost mirrorlike delicacy.

Durable and reliable is this traditional water faucet. The white porcelain caps on each faucet clearly announce "hot" and "cold" as they have to generations of bathers—another example that proves how attractive an original design can be, that some ideas were made to last.

This slick, undulating sink is composed of curved white Mexican tiles that wrap around the basin itself, bend up the back wall for splash space, and flow on down the counter to the wall. These large, highly polished tiles, reflecting light from the two arched windows that frame the mirror, make a firm, heavy-looking sink, reminiscent of an earlier day, when tiles such as these were custom-made. This area is tough and durable, and complements the lighter wood and wicker trim of the cabinet space beneath.

Like chess pieces poised for the crucial move, these stylish faucets from Zazzeri of Florence may capture the needs of many modern basins, where strikingly new colors are desired to match a traditional design. At once contemporary and yet conventional, these faucets will add a bright touch of color to coordinate with other aspects of the overall designs.

This rich interior of soft yellow lamplight and deep gold and ocher gently lures the guest into a room warm and luxurious. The smooth bulge of a mosaic basin curves out to meet the user. The dark washbowl itself, like a deep shadow cast by the mirror, accents the darker tones of the mosaic counter. In a room so quiet, so subdued, the rich gold mirror frame, lamp fixtures, and water taps are all the decorative touches that are really necessary. The lamplight reflected in the mottled wallpaper lends a mysterious depth to the wall's design; gently strengthened, the light gleams off the points of gold that enwreath this dark basin like a sapphire ringed by precious jewels.

This Italian washbasin reflects the space-age penchant for streamlined modules that contain individualized compartments for accoutrements and those electronic "extras" that give space-traveling dreamers their finely tuned sense of control. The ensemble contains a digital clock and a radio for music, weather reports, traffic patterns, and the precise moment of day when morning grooming must end and the dash to meet deadlines begins. Four revolving boxes loaded with accessories, two on each side of the mirror, are easy to reach, and rotate smoothly into obscurity. A round magnifying mirror has its own cup to hold cosmetics, and built-in fluorescent bulbs on each side afford maximum illumination for both sides of the face.

This twin set of octagonal toilet and bidet is elegantly capped with seats and fixtures of gunmetal. The interior bowls are also gunmetal, giving both units a firm, satisfying appearance of cleanliness and endurance. The canister base of each fixture, sitting solidly on the white tile, seems to emerge as part of the floor itself. The marbled band that trims both toilet and bidet is a decorous clamp to fix them tightly to the wall. A perfect study in purity of line, shape, and material—the geometry of permanence.

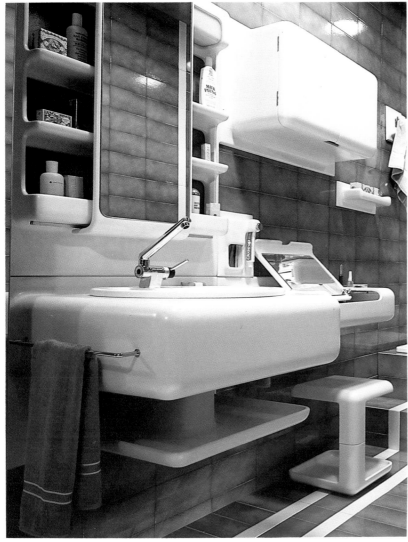

These permanent fixtures made from molded plastic look truly permanent. Of Italian design, this basin, storage cabinet, and make-up stand are made to last. Impressive in bulk and with smooth rounded edges, these white fixtures boldly accent the gray and maroon color combination of the rest of the bathroom. Notice the extra shelf space beneath the basin. The pop-up mirrow on the cosmetic table folds down, thus creating another smooth table surface to work on. In a style not compatible with every bathroom, these fixtures demand a large open space to accommodate their massive presence.

This toilet setting preserves the original meaning of the term "water closet." In fact it appears this room was actually a nondescript closet first and a colorful WC second. Not to be deterred by inconvenient plumbing, the designer installed the tank a bit skewed from the usual arrangement. But the law of gravity has never dictated alignment, only motion and direction! The striking red-and-yellow color combination boldly defies the strategy that less-assured designers would probably have adopted, namely, camouflaging the water pipe with some dark-colored paint, not bright yellow. But the personality behind this unique construction obviously takes delight in the originality and ingenuity that have transformed this narrow space into a bright, cheerful, even fun, WC!

Although they may have originated and become popular first on the California coast, just steps from the pounding surf they simulate, hot tubs are now a national phenomenon. This New York hot tub is about as far from the California environment as one can get. Not only is the view urban, it is aerial. Nestled high above the city, this hot-tub owner can satisfy his fantasy for life on both coasts—the soft California redwood tub and the spectacular view of Manhattan. Presumably while dozing in the hammock, this lucky bather might dream of another coast, somewhere miles and hours from California and New York—a deserted tropical island where the hammock is strung between palm trees on a sandy beach that has never known an American fad called "hot tubbing."

They say the healthiest water is from pure mountain streams, the cleanest air is high up near the peaks, and certainly the most spectacular views come from the scenic overlooks that perch precariously above spreading vistas of valleys at sunset. This lucky homeowner enjoys it all from a mountaintop bathroom retreat where a pink marble tub seems to be carved out of the stone itself. The very room, a delicate framework of windows and skylights, could have been chiseled from the cliff. For physical comfort during long baths, the tub's interior has several areas contoured into seats and reclining sections that fit and support the body in more than one position of repose. Truly a spot to celebrate the close of day, a secure private mountain hideaway.

Here is a tub that seems to step from the outdoor world of greenery and open sky into the dark interior world of refuge and privacy. With an iridescent tub of aquamarine tiles, this bathing area shimmers with a wet, pebbly texture suggestive of pure mineral springs. The glass walls and sloped roof that enclose the outdoor section of this tub reach into the fern-laden patio, where fantasies of sylvan nymphs and water sprites can entertain a bather on a long summer afternoon. The fiery toilet-seat cover is a dramatic contrast to the wet, verdant mood of the room—and yet this bathroom is so much a part of the earth that the unity of nature almost demands an expression of heat, a blaze of energy to temper the hushed coolness of the tub and tile.

3

Accessories

This heavy rubber shower curtain reflects not only the controlling design concept of one dominant color—red—but also the thoughtful simplicity that this bathroom offers. Distractions are reduced to a minimum, and the bather is spotlighted in a fiery burst of phoenixlike self-discovery, perhaps even self-renewal, emerging from the glowing red warmth of this bathing chamber. A striking statement about the use of accessories is apparent as you peek into this bathroom. When the major accessories and walls dissolve into a monochromatic background, as they do here, the overall effect spotlights the larger fixtures or special attractions, such as a plant, a basin of water, or you, the bather.

The bathroom presents a challenging paradox. Of all the rooms in the home, it demands unequivocal cleanliness, order, and arrangement because its purpose is to provide the surroundings that let you clean, order, and arrange your physical appearance. And yet how easily after each person uses the bathroom does it begin to reflect the soiled, cluttered disarray that defeats its purpose! A toothpaste smear on the basin, a soggy carpet beside the tub, a wastebasket sprouting soiled tissues and used dental floss, a strand of hair on the drinking cup. All the unavoidable, unpleasant conditions caused by regular bathroom use must be quickly eliminated before the next user, perhaps a guest, enters.

Which brings us to another paradox: filled with the most personal and intimate belongings, the bathroom is shared with others, even nonmembers of the household. Even if a small room, the bath must contain areas for storage and easy access to the numerous accessories that each family member protects and guards so jealously. In a space so personal and yet so communal, what demands of territoriality and private property we make! It's *my* toothbrush, *my* towel, *my* face cloth, *my* hairbrush, *my* turn!

*W*here and how you arrange your bathroom accessories depends on several factors. A large bathroom can readily accommodate a substantial supply of accessories and accoutrements, whereas a small, compact room will require more strategic planning. For instance, where you have a choice of colors, such as in towels, small fixtures, mats, curtains, even tissues, similar colors that either accent the walls and large fixtures or complement them, will create a tidy, more spacious look. It's best not to mix too many

colors and patterns in a small room or you will have a cluttered look even before you add the bottles, jars, brushes, tubes, and other paraphernalia. Also, a room that is unified with a theme, style, or color combination gives the illusion of order and neatness, even in those times when, to your accustomed eye, the mess and dirt are present.

In developing your strategy for accessories, remember to account for the number of people who will regularly use your bathroom, their ages and sexes, their personal habits and hangups. Towel racks, for example, should provide ample space for each member of the family, not only for hanging the towel but for drying it as well. People with shorter arms may need their racks close to the tub or shower so that they can reach them safely without stretching and slipping on a wet surface. Safety requires that towel racks be firmly attached to walls since everyone, kids and adults alike, will grab for them when they slip on the wet floor or tile. Toothbrush holders, soap trays, tissue rollers, mug holders, and, of course, individual mugs, when coordinated in style and color, can draw together a room, creating a unified appearance, especially if they complement the larger fixtures such as tub, basin, and toilet.

*E*very bathroom should have soft touches. While a room of hard, sleek surfaces is easy to clean, the effect may be cold and sterile. A bathroom atmosphere can be softened by a judicious arrangement of towels, mats, curtains, and carpets. There is nothing more luxurious to the body after stepping from the bath or shower than a fluffy, dry, all-embracing bath towel. Although materials are a matter of personal taste, towels that have a large

Since the bathroom can be used for dressing as well as for washing, why not move dressers and wardrobe closer to the bath, basin, cosmetics, and mirrors? Today's living spaces do not rigidly segregate furniture by room as traditional design theories advised in the past. This heavy antique dresser looks almost as if it were custom-made for the narrow space between the basin and the floor-length window. Not only can it store the usual bathroom accessories such as linens, cleansers, brushes, and toiletries, but it can also keep undergarments, socks, handkerchiefs, and small articles of clothing nearby so that dressing can actually begin where bathing leaves off. Notice as well how the light wicker panels in the doors and drawers beneath the sink make a nice contrast to the dark mahogany of the dresser.

amount of natural cotton pile are soft and comforting and offer maximum absorbency. The veloured and sculptured look may add an aesthetic touch, but the flat or embossed side seems to shun water and requires more patting and rubbing to dry the skin. A soft bathmat is a must in any bathroom. If the floor is hard, a mat prevents slipping; if the floor is carpeted, a mat will keep the carpet beside the tub from getting soaked with water running off the body. In winter, carpeted floors are great because they are warm; and dropped bottles and jars won't break as easily, nor will dropped rings, toothpaste caps, contact lenses, and other small items bounce away into corners and behind the toilet, where they are difficult to retrieve. A bathroom carpet, however, must be easy to shampoo and quick-drying, or the floor will soon come to resemble a loathsome swamp. Having both carpeted and noncarpeted areas in the bathroom, if it is large enough, will solve the dilemma of utility versus comfort.

Providing space for accessories is essential, and there should be counters and open shelves within close reach with the paraphernalia most often used: toothbrushes, soaps, shampoos, combs, brushes—and other storage areas for keeping supplies: extra towels, extra soap, additional rolls of paper, etc. Too often these items are placed haphazardly on the basin counter, the rim around the tub, or precarious shelving over the sink, where bottles and other glass objects can easily fall and shatter. Medicine cabinets and cabinets under the basin are the traditional storage areas, and creative use of space can extend them into nontraditional areas. For instance, the medicine cabinet does not have to be over the sink, where items can fall out and break, or where rising too quickly

For that old-fashioned bathtub in an old-fashioned house, these gold-plated accessories add new life and sparkle to the subdued colors and materials of yesteryear. Matching the feet of this tub, the bath rack, fixture ensemble, and towel holder collect all the equipment you need for a bath that is comfortable and nostalgic. The tub rack holds sponges, soap, shampoos, and bath oils. The tap fixture can convert the water spout into a hand-held shower head. All the advantages of a shower in a room whose antique charm would be destroyed by a modern shower installation. A companion set of fixtures and tub rack comes in black chrome for rooms whose basic tones require a striking darker trim.

For an old-time tub along the wall with no apron space on which to set soaps and bottles, accessory wall attachments can be mounted within easy reach. A towel rack, a double cup holder, a soap dish, and the standard tub tray bring all your bathing materials within an arm's length while you soak in your favorite bath oils.

from bending over the basin can crack your head on the door swung partly open. If children share an adult bathroom, drugs and medicines should be kept either out of reach or outside the bathroom altogether. Even if your children are trained not to play with medicines, their friends may not be.

*B*ut don't let your imagination be bathroom-bound. There are fixtures intended for use in other rooms that, when transplanted into the bathroom, offer wonderful storage space. Kitchen or living-room shelving, for books or art objects, for example, might be cleverly utilized in the bathroom.

Hanging baskets can contain soaps, plastic bottles, sponges, loofahs. A simple pole with hooks or an old-fashioned hat rack will let you hang your robe or clean change of clothes while you shower—no need to toss them on the floor or the toilet seat. Speaking of seats, there is always a need for a place to sit down in the bathroom—for drying the feet, performing a pedicure, or just relaxing. A cushioned box can satisfy the need and at the same time conceal storage space. Or high shelving overhead and partially out of sight can stock extra towels and face cloths. An unused window can be remade into handy shelf

space for small items.

Hampers and wastebaskets can be attractive and practical accessories, adding to the overall decor of the bathroom. Although a clothes hamper is not absolutely necessary, it is a convenient item that encourages bathroom users not to leave soiled clothing or dirty towels lying around. A wastebasket should have a flip-up lid to prevent unsightly tissues, cotton swabs, and empty containers from destroying the ambience of cleanliness.

*A*nd then there are the toilet articles themselves! In an age that creates and caters to individual needs and fanta-

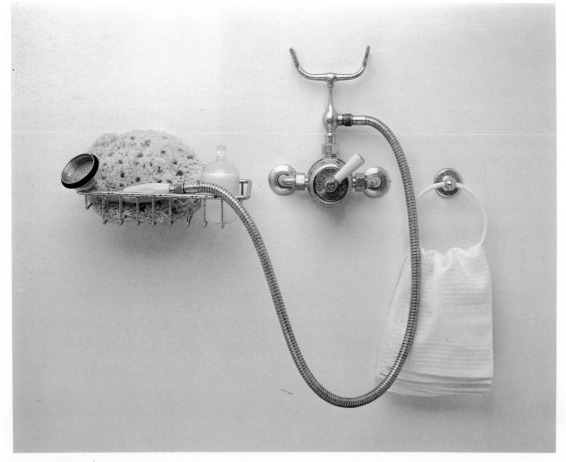

For the tub where you want to enjoy the advantages of a shower or for that rinse area near the pool, or for any washing area where a spray of water would be refreshing, this gold-plated ensemble with white porcelain would be quite stylish. This model comes complete with matching towel rack and soap holder.

sies as ingeniously as ours does, the cosmetics needed for personal appearance become treasured items, endowed with magical properties. The proliferation of products and potions and so-called health and beauty secrets stimulates our imaginations into thinking that we too can transform our face, our age, our shape, and create a new public self as easily as we change hair color or scent. And yet, there is a real sense in which the face we put on—"a face to meet the other faces that you meet," as poet T.S. Eliot wrote—*is* who we are, at least to other people. Personal appearance does indeed reflect personality. Virtue, strength of character, and self-confidence radiate from the eyes, the face, and skin, even though we know these qualities are more than skin deep. And so the decisions about personal toilet articles: natural, herbal, fortified, chemically treated, pH-balanced, unscented, scented, lightly scented, new, lemon, improved, unbreakable container, childproof caps, travel size, family size, mint flavor, natural flavor, unflavored, not to mention the hexas-, tetras-, polys-, and other unsaturated -ines, -ides, -izes, and -odes. Odes? Yes, someone is sure to write an ode, someday, somewhere, to . . . What will it be? Beauty? Health? Or Fantasy?

Wood and brass highlight this bathroom. While the major fixtures are constructed of deep cherry wood, the light fixtures, towel racks, and taps are highly polished brass that gleams pleasantly against the dark wood and sober wall color. The cluster of lights over the tub makes a convenient reading area, while the brass-colored headrest invites long soaks with a favorite book. The freestanding towel rack can be moved closer to the tub if needed or left snugly next to the sink. Notice the stylish soap and cup holder, also made of brass.

This washing area tastefully exploits its dual color combination by a selection of white accessories to match the pedestal basin. Towel racks, a shelf, and light fixtures incorporate the same simple design, which adds trim, narrow lines of white to the dominant gray-blue background of the room. The plain white lampshades for either side of the mirror balance the fixtures. Notice the painted tiles scattered at unexpected points on the wall, each a dark-blue pot holding a leafy green plant. An example of how a room limited to two colors can hold the interest with minor subtle touches.

The trap door of this toiletry cabinet conceals an assortment of cosmetics much the way a child's toy chest hides a mess of playthings. Indeed, it caters to the childlike love of secret compartments that stays with us even into adulthood. Simply constructed of naturally finished wood, this lift-up door holds the grooming mirror fastened on its underside and unleashes the cluster of toilet articles that would not harmonize with the vigorous patterns of the wallpaper. The nervous effect of these walls is smartly tempered with calming wooden cabinets and basin counters that provide ample elbow room. The frenzied array of bottles and jars is relegated to a hideaway drawer, thus maintaining the intriguing tension between movement and stability.

This slim and elegant toothbrush holder is ideal for design arrangements in which you wish to leave the walls uncluttered. One advantage to a countertop toothbrush rack is that it can be removed as your needs dictate. For example, on occasions when guests will be using the bathroom, you may want to store some accessories, such as toothbrushes, to give the room a less utilitarian look. A toothbrush rack like this one is easily removed for the evening, creating space for cut flowers or candles.

Here is an example of how accessories can highlight color choice and design statement. Determined to make the bathroom both decorative and functional, this homeowner has displayed the most mundane items on a wicker-wrapped free-standing shelf. Each jar, bottle, canister, brush, or stack of towels becomes an additional decorative touch. Both the wicker basket and the shelves complement the woven pattern on the wallpaper. The beautiful shag rug on the floor adds a touch of warmth, its many colors and deep textures harmonizing with the towels and linens so casually exposed.

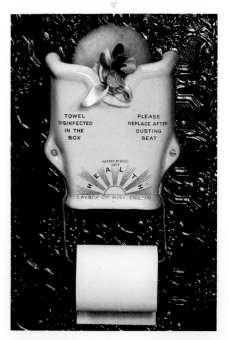

Patented at the turn of the century, this antique toilet-paper dispenser with its built-in toilet seat buffer is the dispossessed grandparent of the unimaginative paper seat covers found in today's commercial establishments. With an eye to both good health and good looks, a modern bather can use this charming porcelain accessory to evoke the gentler amenities of an earlier day. Who of that pre–World War I generation realized he would fight to make the world safe for paper toilet-seat covers—or worse, the paper sani-strip that must be ripped from the seat before the toilet can be used?

Flowers and herbs. The scent of nature's own sweet fragrances mingle with the pine of this bathroom for an experience that brings back the pleasures and smells of an earlier day. The array of accessories in this little spot perfectly reflects the owner's appreciation of the traditional domestic pastimes. Even this wall basin has only a single tap for cold water. A person who can wait while thistle and sunflowers dry undoubtedly has the patience to live with a single tap. As the herbal calendar on the wall should warn us, here live people whose lives are tuned to the seasons of planting, growth, and harvest, lives that are not hurried from April to May to June.

For the sleek, uncluttered look, wall cabinets like these can conceal a multitude of cleaning materials and extra supplies. When closed, the fold-down doors create hauntingly mysterious panels to match other black trim in the room such as the whimsical sea mural painted on the raised tank. When opened, bowl cleaners, brushes, extra towels, and cloths, not to mention additional rolls of toilet paper, pop handily into view. Similar cabinets of varying sizes mounted on other walls turn this bathroom into a study in black and white—a stark but striking combination well suited to the bath and easily maintained for hygiene and aesthetic appeal. Here is an almost magical way to dispense with the cosmetics and paraphernalia that can distract in a bathroom whose overall scheme is simplicity and spareness.

4

Decorative Touches

The bathing alcove off this elegantly furnished bedroom is a miniature world of classical antiquity. Framed by two Corinthian columns, the sunken bath sits serenely at the base of an alabaster pedestal. The woman sculpted in smooth, creamy marble has the noble bearing of someone who has visited the major spas of the Mediterranean and now prepares to step into the waters, here, where she is at home, in rooms whose very color and texture exude a sweet feminine perfume, redolent with peach blossoms and berries. A mirror behind the bathing area creates depth and suggests that there is more here than meets the eye, more than just one sunken tub, one woman, one afternoon. A fountain perhaps? A sculpture garden? Or another hidden room, draped with sheer peach-colored curtains in which ancient pastimes might be reinstated for patrician guests who cultivate the arts of friendship and eroticism.

A room designed for applying the finishing touches to your personal appearance should itself have pleasant finishing touches. Decorative touches. Aesthetic touches. Even the most utilitarian bathroom can be transformed into an experience of art and poetry by well-placed objects and splashes of color that delight the eye and stimulate the imagination. Interior design for the bathroom can be accomplished in several ways: the display of bona fide art objects, such as sculpture, framed prints, mobiles; the use of practical items chosen for their aesthetic impact in color or shape, such as towels, sponges, soaps, mirrors, or a comb and brush "burst" on the wall; or simply by a thoughtful selection of color and design in materials used on walls, floors, and fixtures.

*P*otted plants have invaded our homes in great profusion recently in our efforts to bring the feeling of the fresh outdoors inside, and there's no reason why the bath should not have its own share of greenery. What better environment than the steamy atmosphere of a bathroom for the sensuously delicate fern? Move your spider plants into the bath and watch their long tendrils shoot forth with new growth. A multiwindowed room can become a lush solarium when filled with flowering plants that require a bright, humid environment. If your bathroom is not well lighted by natural light, there are plants that require little light or do well under artificial light. There are even mysterious plants that grow in the dark. A bathroom can quickly assume a lush tropical effect when many plants are present, creating a miniature jungle; but if you are not the type who longs for the return to nature, one or two carefully cultivated plants can enhance a bathroom

Try pulling yourself together in this bathroom where the wall literally has "ears," and the tub a "body" with a real shower "head," and the sink has "legs" although not its own and not standing on them. There are helping "hands" waiting at strategic places and "arms" to lean on should the disorienting effect of this room induce you into a genuine out-of-the-body experience. But who says every bathroom must be restful? This tumultuous setting roars with distractions and reminders that beneath the face we paint on is another person—hopefully genuine, authentic, and with greater depth than the cardboard artist who seems to take pride in the eclecticism her art has wrought.

Here is eclecticism with a more traditional ring—if ring is the word! Gray and white squares checkering the walls and tub; taffeta fabric ribbing the ceiling to catch the upward thrust of light from the Corinthian cornstalk lampstands; a bust of a golden-helmeted, golden-bosomed Amazon; a coral bouquet to complement the floral design of the Queen Ann chairs; a larger wicker trunk and wicker basket for the potted plant; and the double sunburst mirror above the tub observing it all like the great omniscient eye of some Aztec deity. A veritable potpourri of times and places in which jars, tubes, and canisters huddle defensively on an island table top against the majestic centuries that sweep across this room.

in a quiet, civilized fashion. In fact, a single plant to complement your basic color scheme might be all you need.

Don't overlook the decorative effect of pots. Clay pots are soft, porous, earth-colored, almost native to a warm, steamy atmosphere, especially as they complement other natural, earth tones in the room. On the other hand, an electric-red or -blue plastic pot will go well in a modern bathroom dominated by brightly colored plastic fixtures. For more refined tastes, there are elegant planters for bathrooms with a studied, classical look. When thinking of plants, remember that a spray of cut flowers will add beauty and fragrance to any bathroom on special occasions, for guests.

Sea souvenirs, such as shells, pieces of coral, and driftwood, are favorite items that seem to belong in a bathroom. Either displayed on the wall, clustered on a counter, or trimming the tub, these gifts from the sea are natural reminders of the watery regions from which we once emerged. A half-conscious memory of soothing waves, bracing salt air, and healthy sunshine can be a psychic tonic to refresh the mind and mobilize the body. A simple glass jar of any size can hold a collection of baby shells. A larger shell can be both decorative and practical when used as a soap dish, an ashtray, or a catchall for rings and other jewelry.

*M*agical aesthetic effects can be achieved with mirrors, and what more logical room for mirrors than the bath? You will have to determine, of course, how often you wish to face your nude body and how much of it you enjoy observing. Somewhere between narcissistic voyeurism and puritanical denial is the perfect number and arrangement of mirrors. If your bathroom is

small, mirrors strategically placed will create the illusion of depth and additional space. Wherever they hang, they will reflect light, color, and movement. If your bathroom is dimly lighted because of a small window, a mirror will increase the illumination from it, especially helpful behind a plant that requires extra light to grow. The "infinity effect" produced by mirrors placed facing each other has become popular in modern bathrooms, possibly because the multiplication of light, color, and body reflections, like a moving kaleidoscope, overcomes the empty feeling of a bathroom when you are all alone in it.

*T*he total design for your bathroom must include a judicious use of light, especially for creating a variety of moods and intensities. Tinted bulbs in attractive fixtures radiate softer, alternative lighting patterns from the harsh, honest light you need for grooming. Candles can achieve the same restful effect, and they're attractive even when unlighted. Candle glow makes an inviting welcome light for evening guests, and scented candles eliminate unpleasant odors. During a bath, one simple flame flickering quietly in the room can provide a soothing focal point for meditation and romantic experiences. In addition to candles, old-fashioned lanterns and hurricane lamps produce the same restful mood and offer just the right amount of light for middle-of-the-night visits when the full light would wake you up more than is necessary. If your room is high-tech, you might consider a simple—or crazy—piece of neon to add color, light, and mood. A single neon light of dark color makes a great nightlight.

*A*t once decorative and practical, wicker baskets can solve the problem

This potpourri of styles, accessories, and patterns is a fine example of how the eclectic can indeed create a unified and appealing look. The Japanese silk kimono hanging over the tub lends an air of Oriental extravagance. "Men" and "Ladies" signs are playfully attached over each of the saloon doors leading to smaller rooms on each side of the bath. A collection of cut glass enhances the magnificent wooden dais and shelf space around the tub, each piece becoming a classy companion for the bottles and jars of toilet articles that line the shelves and also contribute to the overall effect. The clothes tree on the wall sports a wide-brimmed sombrero, a feathered cloak, a silk gown, and a white boa. A splendid skylight in the high ceiling floods the bathing area with natural daylight, while a neat row of backstage dressing-room lights trims and illuminates the grooming section of this spacious room.

of decorating an empty space with a minimum of trouble and expense. The natural fiber of wicker, associated with tropical climates, goes well in most bathrooms. Either hanging from the ceiling, arranged on the walls, or placed on the floor in a corner, they're attractive and useful. In fact, ordinary bathroom accessories kept in one or two wicker baskets can add color and life to areas where a more elaborate decor would be out of place. For example, colored bars of soap or rolls of different colored tissue can be arranged haphazardly in a basket to brighten an unexciting corner. A heap of sponges or loofahs looks good in wicker, as do brightly colored washcloths, rolled up like dinner napkins, offering a clean choice to each guest. Wastebaskets and clothes hampers made from wicker are less obtrusive when they blend with other wicker elements, such as a chair or a low stool.

*W*hen selecting framed prints, wallpaper, and curtains or shades or shutters, think beyond the traditional bathroom designs. A plain bathroom can become a circus of color and charac-

ters, depending on the themes and patterns you choose. A corny, clownish poster adds humor. An erotic print or a framed *Playboy* cartoon can make a sensuous statement to intrigue your guests. Or have your window curtains and shades personally designed with the characters and events from your favorite fantasies or historical eras.

*M*ost of all, the bathroom does not need to be ordinary when it comes to aesthetics. Use it as a gallery for photographs or sculpture. Arrange family portraits and candid shots of relatives taken at various rites of passage. After all, the bathroom is a private room where one is constantly confronted with the passage of time and its effects upon the face, body, and hair. What more private group of faces to share it with than your loved ones? Either arranged on the wall, or standing in frames on a counter or shelf, old photos bring companionship, reverie, and fond memories for the moments alone. Of course, some people may not be able to tolerate the ancestral stare at their nude bodies, and may thus prefer old daguerreotypes of other people's

families, anonymous faces picked up at flea markets or auctions.

The bathroom is a wonderful space for small pieces of sculpture, especially classical nudes and mythological characters. When placed in front of a mirror, a piece of sculpture can be viewed in the round, something not always possible in other rooms. And what better celebration of the human body than to be surrounded by original works or reproductions of the great and famous bodies from the historical and mythical past?

Whatever approach you take, be it expensive objects selected from the best galleries or natural souvenirs brought home from a jaunt through the woods or along a beach, the bathroom should not be neglected and relegated to the status of a utility room. It demands beauty and character. *You* demand beauty and character. A simple touch or an elaborate plan. An exotic art object of great price or a cluster of dried stalks. With insight and bold thinking, you can find the finishing touches that will turn a dull, lifeless bathroom into a room of tasteful imagery inviting enjoyment.

Our humanity in common with people the world over is stated here in this scrubbed-tile nook beneath the skylight and dangling vines. Heads and faces of several colors and races are represented in this corner, where our chief concern is with our own face and the appearance it will make in the outside world. From very primitive clay tutelaries on the counter to the distinguished bust of modern man across from them, the long history of human grooming rituals is enshrined here. Like the carnival masks decorating the wall, our own faces are often just as painted and stylized for the proper occasion, the special festival, or the ineluctable deception that begins here, at the sink, in a moment of plain truth.

A simple, round, black tub. An irresistible heap of pillows clustered casually at the edge. Marvelously huge green-leafed plants reflected in a mirror. And wood fixtures that panel the wall and frame the window. A bathroom decorated primarily by just a few common objects—pillows and plants—but exuberant in hypnotic color. Notice how perfectly the dark green and black, the red and orange, the burnt and burnished textures of the materials, captivate one's sense of comfort. Here is a bath that guarantees comfort and relaxation. A room to mesmerize the bather, a spot frozen in a moment of intense enjoyment that you wish could go on forever—where even the ceramic duck is immobilized by the sheer ease with which this room seduces.

The Tao of washing is a subject little discussed but much considered at this white porcelain basin. Greeted by a smiling Buddha each morning and night, the owner of this bathroom can, like monks and mystics, contemplate the repetitious patterns of the universe, such as the unending dance of soot and soap, the ultimate futility of trying to scrub one's skin clean, the meaning of that last gargle. What is the sound of one sud bursting?

As decorative touches and room dividers, these large, sprawling plants create a junglelike effect, a moment of wildness in a room quite civilized with cosmetics, frosted glass panels in elegantly carved Gothic frames and two photographs mounted high, near the ceiling. In this bathroom, the spreading tendrils of vines and fan-shaped leaves can climb wantonly over the brass poles without the fear that either the room or its occupants will revert to a state of wildness. Or if so, then only for that pure moment when the human form returns to its own roots to wash and splash and prepare for the evolution back into modern society.

This sun-splashed bathroom is decorated primarily by the wicker furniture that clusters naturally on the Navaho rug and whose finely woven strands present a different texture and durability from the smooth slate tiles that step up from the bright floor to the tub alcove. Notice how wonderfully the dimly shimmering candlelight and the reflected play of the sun in the chair backs and table add new dimensions of light and shadow. Here is a room that invites you to linger alone and contemplate the movement of time and sunlight, or to share the relaxed moments after a bath with a friend or lover. It's a space for coffee, conversation, and flowers.

The rose and coral color theme is judiciously exploited throughout the room with smaller objects such as towels, blinds, flowers, even the carefully selected prints that adorn the walls. The ample use of mirrors around the tub, including on the ceiling, shapes and folds the basic color into other regions of the room. Even the translucent vase and ashtray present no obstruction to diffusing the dominant color throughout. In a room so unified by a single color, even a bath towel slung over the edge of the tub with seeming carelessness becomes a pinpoint of purpose and design rather than an indicator of clutter. The Norwegian rose marble pattern also exudes a scatter effect that races to the far corners of a room, stretching even farther into the mirrors. An exciting example of how mirrors not only reflect reality but also the recesses of the imagination.

These slick bathroom fixtures radiate from a central pillar of smoked mirror into a room spare in color and mysteriously deep in the black recesses of the mirrored walls. The stark contrast between black casements for the tub and plumbing and the white porcelain of the bowls, basin, and tub itself gives this room a strong aura of light and shadow, clarity and smoke. The elevated lighting cube is reflected in the mirrors high above the head, almost as if it hovered there, defying gravity. The reconciliation of opposites in this bathroom is truly stunning. The smooth, sleek panels, by reflecting the softer textures of the Berber carpet, curtain, and straw, create an environment almost subconsciously unified in its polarities.

A bathroom such as this one, shooting outward at contrary angles, almost demands the haphazard ambience created by such varied objects of art and nature—sculptured pieces, framed paintings and posters, artificial flowers between a cluster of rocks on the one side and corked glass jars on the other. The playfulness of this room reaches out into the patio, where the wooden fence becomes a bulletin board for favorite clippings, changeable with the seasons or moods. Approaching the bathtub, you enter another world, step up, step down, and in. Hold tight to the two built-in handgrips as you lie back and with the toys of your adult years recapture those childhood urges to go outside and play.

Some bathrooms make it on one or two precious objects placed so as to command attention and admiration. A few rooms stun their visitors with an utter starkness that cannot be troubled by even one or two decorative touches. Then there are bathrooms like this one, which seems to grab visitors and implore them to linger awhile and notice the gallery of clutter that breathes friendliness and camaraderie. This bathroom, furnished with photographs, paintings, and prints, announces joyfully that a total life can be located here, not just for the few hours a day that bathing or brushing hair may take. Other times, other places, old faces, memories, special fantasies are on display; and the guest is invited to peruse them, and return with fresh insights into his or her host.

5

What's It Doing Here?

Scavenging through antique shops on weekends might turn up a handsomely preserved barber chair such as this one. Such items can pose design problems for many rooms, but how natural it looks in this distinctive bathroom where dense foliage and coarsely woven pillows ring the tub. What makes this room work so perfectly is that all the objects are of an imposing bulk—the wide tub with a shallow, contoured lounge level and a deeper plunge space, the large, heavy-fibered pillows, and the enormous dracaena growing so heartily at the corner. Even the window is of a span to match the room, allowing a wooded view for the wet bather to contemplate from the secure embrace of the barber chair.

There is a world of surprises beyond the bath. This necessary room, once considered an aesthetic wasteland, has in recent years taken on a life of its own, far removed from the simple bodily demands it formerly satisfied in such drab and sterile surroundings. Today's homeowners and apartment dwellers are turning the bathroom into a multipurpose room to accommodate other daily duties as well as frivolous hobbies and playful pastimes. Especially in these times when economy of resources dictates a judicious and ecologically sensitive use of materials and space, designers and do-it-yourselfers are discovering the many varied uses for the room that was long ago called "the necessary." As the 1980s progress, home design and apartment renovation will incorporate strikingly bold ideas for transforming the bath into a playroom, workroom, and leisure room all in one. You may discover yourself exclaiming more frequently as you enter a new bathroom: "What's *this* doing here?!"

*I*t doesn't take years of studying interior design to figure out that among the rooms in the house where a telephone would be most handy is the bathroom. In fact, it is already one of those unproven and ultimately unprovable verities of folk wisdom that the way to assure a long-awaited phone call is to step into the shower and lather up or slouch comfortably into a tub drawn to perfect temperature. In the past, we have devised makeshift methods to ambush the disturbing call or to receive it as graciously as possible. Some people take the phone off the hook or flip on the answering machine. Others install phones with long cords that will reach into the bathroom, and hope they remember to bring the phone in before getting into the tub. Stoics just ignore the ringing until it stops. But most people mutter a curse, grab a towel, and drip out to the kitchen or bedroom where, in their most insouciant voice, they answer the blasted phone cheerfully. But why not a phone in the bathroom? Not only can you receive calls, you can make those long, languid conversations to friends and loved ones from the privacy of the tub, the quiet of the bathroom, the one total escape room in the entire house. Here you can visualize the person to whom you are speaking without the unnecessary distractions and interruptions that seem to occur by the minute in other rooms.

*R*emember how Dad used to stack the last three issues of *Reader's Digest* on the tank of the toilet? By size, format, and length of article, this venerable bible of the "quick read" always made it from the mailbox to the bathroom in a matter of hours. But why just a handful of *Reader's Digests*? Why not a library of your favorite books and magazines, light reading, joke books, the classics you enjoy browsing through every now and then? Bookshelves and magazine racks can be permanent and attractive fixtures of any bathroom. If you plan to stock expensive volumes, however, enclosed shelves will be necessary to protect them against steam or spray from the shower. And while you're at it, rig up a decent reading light over the tub, safely mounted so it won't fall into the bathwater. Then stock up. Add your latest magazines, the escape novels of adventure and romance that advertise themselves as the books "for your quiet moments alone," the encyclopedias and fact books, and the Sunday supplements that you didn't have time to read on the busy weekend. Then lie back, relax, and let the mind

The owner of this bathroom knows the importance of following physical exertion with periods of recuperation. In a room large enough to maintain a strenuous regimen, there is also ample space for reclining, cooling down, drying off beads of perspiration. The soothing, restful blue tiles can calm the excited nerves as the body relaxes. As more and more people learn the value of a regular program of physical exercise for total well-being, home exercise rooms like this one will become more common. A generation or two ago most home workout equipment was relegated to a corner of the basement or an unused area of the garage; the home of the future will undoubtedly incorporate physical fitness gear into the bathroom, which will then become truly a "body room."

Here is a special kids' bathroom that should thrill the heart of the child privileged to show it off to neighborhood chums as "my bathroom!" A bright circus of puppets, dolls, and stuffed animals in a low-ceilinged room that increases the stature of the elfin bathers who use it. Built in one of those unused corners on the top floor, this red-and-blue bathroom could function equally as a second playroom on rainy days when kids are confined indoors. A well-stocked room with extra storage space over the tub artfully concealed behind the fabric murals, here a child could play and dream for hours while listening to the rain patter on the roof just overhead.

soak up its own nourishment even as your body soaks in the warm, relaxing waters of the bath.

*A*s our increasingly sedentary life-style drives more and more of us to the jogging tracks, racquetball courts, aerobics classes, and Nautilus gyms, the bathroom should become what it indeed is meant to be: the body room. In a bathroom of ample size, there is room for exercise equipment such as stationary bicycles, free weights, slant boards, chinning bars, full-length mirrors for stretching and yoga, and much more. Exercise in the bath, and you're only a step or two away from the workout to the shower, from sweaty panting to that first invigorating gasp under a bracing cold spray of water. If space permits, add a cooling-off area with lounge and sunlamp, and numerous thick towels. Even if you can't find space for equipment in the bathroom, you could convert one end of the bathroom into a rest area in which to collapse and relax after outdoor exercise. On hand should be lotions, oils, and deep-heat rubs for the unavoidable aches and minor injuries that accompany the strenuous life.

*W*here every square foot is precious, as in apartments, the bathroom might also serve as a laundry room with the new compact washer-drier combinations that are designed and manufactured precisely for limited space. The bathroom is a room ready-made for washing clothes, already on the water line with pipes, drains, and other plumbing. All it takes to transform your personal washroom into your clothes washroom are the right appliances. If you match their color with the major fixtures of the room (tub, toilet, wash basin), the washer and drier then become part of the

overall scheme. If you can't match, or open appliances would detract from your aesthetic design, hide them away in linen closets or build cabinets around them. Even if a washer-drier cannot be fitted into your bathroom, you can always purchase fashionable clothes racks or designer hooks for stretching a clothes line. Then when you wash your fine garments by hand, you will have a space to hang them up to dry—an ideal arrangement for apartment dwellers without basement facilities or yard space.

*I*f you spend a good deal of time in your bathroom, why not install audio and video equipment to enrich your leisure hours? Sound strange? There was a time when the television was relegated solely to the living room or TV room, but now it has become a standard feature at the foot of many beds. Why not pioneer electronic gadgetry in the bathroom? After all, a simple radio is a loyal companion in the morning while you're getting ready for the day ahead. Hear the weather report, keep track of traffic snarls, skim the top of the news reports, continue listening to your favorite morning disc jockey even after you leave the bedroom. If you can't turn your bathroom into a full-scale "media room," you might consider running speakers into it from your stereo system in another room. What Bo Derek did for *Bolero,* you might do for Handel's *Water Music!*

*N*ext: hobbies. Photography, for example, needs a darkroom and a water supply. If your bathroom is a small, dimly lighted room with a minimum of windows, keep your developing equipment there in a special cabinet and work area. Other arts and crafts need sinks, supplies of water, or a

This children's bathroom is not "somewhere over the rainbow" but beneath a whole galaxy of them! The bright, repetitive pattern on the wallpaper is just the thing to mesmerize curious minds. Kids will scrutinize each area for hours, searching for subtle differences only they can see: a tiny smudge here, a bump there, the rude interruption by a window or corner. A mesh net of toys is handy, containing the obligatory rubber critters for the tub and simple push-and-pull toys. The soft childproofing carpet, in the young imagination, can become a green summer lawn for the trees and homes on the wall.

room whose floors are easily cleaned. If the room is already spacious, consider creating a play area in the bathroom for your hobbies. If you are designing your home from scratch (the ultimate hobby!), reconsider the bathroom and turn even just a corner of it into a play or hobby area. Or attack the problem in reverse: add a bathroom to a multiroom complex that is intended for photography, carpentry, hobbies, or exercise.

Some bathrooms would make great kids' rooms with a little imaginative redecoration. Not only should you have storage space for the tub toys, but also you could convert the entire bathroom into an additional nursery for toddlers. Extensive childproofing must render the bathroom as safe as possible. Carpets should cover the hard floor surfaces. Potentially dangerous accessories that might hurt a child, such as glass bottles, scissors, and other pointed objects, should be removed. Once the bathroom is as safe as the other rooms your children play in, you'll discover that spills and accidents will be easy to wipe up and the fixtures and furniture of most bathrooms are indestructible. Of course, this doesn't mean you should lock the child in the bathroom to get the little tyke out of the way. But when the child learns that the bath is an alternative play space, then you can rest assured that steep stairs, hot stoves, costly living-room furniture, and expensive carpets will be far removed from the mischief of pudgy fingers. In a bright, airy, cheerful bathroom, the young child could be as happy as in the official nursery, which we might discover isn't half the fun we adults think it is, if we polled infants and toddlers themselves!

If the trend of the future is toward multipurpose living spaces, we will probably see more exercise bathrooms, media bathrooms, hobby bathrooms, and bed bathrooms...and who knows what else? By the end of the century, you may discover that the spare, lean, traditional bathroom has become a rarity. And instead of asking, "What's it doing here?" the question will be: "Do you mean your bathroom doesn't have a...? Imagine!"

The ambience of a barroom in a private men's club pervades this bathroom. The pub mirror over the bath advertises Pale and Burton Ales. The dark walls and handsome reading lights invite the pursuit of serious study, light browsing, or just distracted ruminating over the world's problems. For more mindless evenings or at a late hour when thought processes grind to a halt, the compact television can be switched on for replays of the day's top sporting events. The stool beside the tub would be an attractive addition in any exclusive clubroom, and, the polished brass rail around the tub, although it's a little high, offers the same kind of support that has kept many a philosopher's foot from slipping off the deep end while lost in the suds of thought.

Here is a quiet, undisturbed retreat for the professional man or woman who returns from a day of meetings, public-affairs engagements, or stressful deadlines. A room to slip out of the public persona, slip into one's basic skin, and then into a tub of hot water for an hour or two of frivolous entertainment and relaxation. The portable television set on the corner of the tub brings favorite evening programs right into the bath. A handy stack of magazines at the elbow will suffice on evenings when there's nothing good on the tube. An executive's escape hatch, minimally furnished to minimize distractions—a place to unwind and de-stress.

A small alcove in or off your bathroom can be converted into anything with a little imagination. This one has been transformed for several uses. Instead of having paint or paper on the walls, this alcove is brightly textured with a large collection of men's ties. Sliding Plexiglas doors protect the fabrics from steam and dust. A silver-plated oval mirror rests on the shelf, for tying and adjusting the Windsor knot. A gallery of old family photographs lends human warmth and approval to the scion who assembles his attire here each morning. An eccentric touch is the display of pincers, tweezers, and scissors. Are they heirlooms, perhaps, handed down from generation to generation and still under the protective eye of his ancestors? Or was it just an uncontrollable urge to display a fine collection of... well, pincers, tweezers, and scissors?

Economy of space and color characterizes this narrow bathroom, and yet there is room here for extras. The bright reds and blues in the wallpaper are so finely lined, they don't compete with the open beige background needed to create the illusion of a larger space. The sink is recessed into the wall so as not to obtrude into the gangway. But conservation of space has not eliminated the need to keep favorite reading materials handy. The trim single file of books above the toilet lends another stripe of color. And because this room is in a remote wing of the house, an extra extension phone on the wall guarantees that time spent here will not be interrupted by the need to dash to another room to answer calls.

In this country cottage the bathroom serves as a laundry, thus conserving much-needed space for other family activities on weekend outings. The double washer-drier unit is stacked to utilize what would be wasted area above the appliances were they located side by side. There's even room left over near the ceiling for an old-fashioned wicker clothes basket.

The sink, conveniently located next to the laundry appliances, has ample storage space beneath it for towels and detergents. In the traditional country style, the storage area has been left open. Rural honesty, devoid of pretense, does not require utilities to be camouflaged or prettified.

In this converted loft apartment across from the Smithfield Meat Market in London's East End, we find this spacious high-tech bedroom that houses the bath in a compact unit styled after the galley of a cruise ship. Behind the two doors with porthole windows are two separate facilities. On the left is a shower room with a white tile interior. The right door leads to a washroom and toilet area. Not shown in this view are the home video equipment center, off to the left, and the large dressing area, on the right. In this roomy and minimally furnished space composed of distinct areas, the queen-sized bed nestles against the wall, covered simply with an orange spread, and shares the corner with a low table, a phone, and a vase of flowers to add a touch of the sensuous to the rigorous design.

As you wander around this spacious London bathroom with tall windows overlooking a residential street, it becomes clear that the peace and repose needed for bathing, reading, or study can be found here. The tub was added to the middle of the study floor. The bookshelves are an unconventional furnishing, and the desk beneath the double window now functions as a dressing table. While the arrangement might be nontraditional, each item itself goes back to an earlier age, and the overall effect, both aesthetically and functionally, works.

In this multi-functional room, you could easily fill many pleasant hours reading mysteries, writing letters, contemplating the day's events before they become diary entries. Most of all, as you spend time here, you learn to appreciate the importance of a room that pleases the life of the mind as well as the needs of the flesh.

For sheer self-indulgence on a wintry day, a hot bath followed by a lazy drying-off period in front of a roaring fire is just the thing. Sip a hot buttered rum while you're wrapped in a towel or a robe, and you can forget the snowy weather outside. This homeowner kept the fireplace when converting this large room of an old house into a bathroom. The eclectic pieces include a Chippendale mirror, brass candlesticks, eighteenth century portraits, and an adjustable standing mirror complete with brush holders. It opens to full length when you need to inspect your entire figure, or it slides to a smaller size when you wish to sit and apply make-up or brush your hair.

Formerly a bedroom in an Edwardian house in London, this bathroom now offers the amenities of comfort, charm, and utility. The main attraction is obviously the old working fireplace, kept in good condition by the owner, who tired of chilly baths in a drafty country home. The roaring fire is a comfy addition to bathing on damp foggy mornings. An array of white English pottery graces the mantel, right at home in a room devoted to a basic white and porcelain character. Notice the combination heater and towel rack on the left of the fireplace. Even on days when a fire is too much trouble, these towels will feel warm and toasty as they heat up, courtesy of the home's central heating system. Close to the towel rack is a cluster of 1920s clothes racks with Art Deco heads on metal shoulder frames.

In this bathroom, a person could profitably enjoy hours of exercise and entertainment and never realize how time flies—a room so inviting, so self-indulgent, so perfect for the time one owes oneself. The universal gym will keep the body well toned and trim for an admirable physique and years of enduring health. The shower and relaxation area awaits the post-exercise period. And the home media center on the far wall can bring favorite music either on cassettes or radio, as well as taped video programs or television specials on the video screen. Various lighting modes can generate a spectrum of moods—track lighting to illuminate the exercise area, recessed lamps along the wall, and even candlelight for periods of relaxation or "easy listening."

6

Unusual Spaces

This bathroom almost reaches back to the days when the "facilities" were located outdoors. But what grandeur! Grandpa never had latrines as plush as this! Literally built outside the house, this bathroom of deep earth colors is open to the sky above and yet decorated with a quality of furniture one would not expect to find in such proximity to nature. In spite of its exposed airiness, the privacy and intimate character of the room are preserved by means of the brick wall, the richly patterned floor, and the elegance each fixture and furnishing lends to the total effect.

The problem with the ordinary is precisely that: it's ordinary. The bathroom is one of the last rooms to escape the fate of being just a commonplace room. Almost as if we anticipate how unexciting a bathroom can be, we peek surreptitiously into a stranger's medicine cabinet or deftly snoop behind the shower curtain in hopes of discovering some secret, some scandal, some surprise, anything that will lift the trip to the bathroom out of the commonplace.

There was a time when a sunken tub was unusual and fascinating, sparking wonderment in inexperienced visitors who imagined how it must feel, how it must work, if indeed it did work like a regular tub! But today sunken tubs are becoming more commonplace, as are raised tubs, Jacuzzis, and the wraparound windows that at one time made a bathroom wall so daring. It takes a forceful stretch of the imagination to conceive a truly unusual bathroom. The generous use of mirrors can surprise many guests; nonbathroom items, such as television sets and exercise equipment, that are slowly staking out their claims for bathroom space still startle and surprise. But perhaps the most engaging quality of an unusual space is not the wall-to-wall mirror, not the window on the world, not the typewriter and filing cabinet next to the bidet, but the innovative adaptation of space, the creative use of what already exists, the satisfying conversion of a *space* into a true *bathroom space*.

Sometimes the location marks a bathroom as unique or unusual. The unexpected lavatory or guest bath built unassumingly onto a wide landing of a staircase. The outdoor shower and rinse area by the pool or patio that saves your guests from tracking sand and water through the house. A special

Here is a bathing-and-recreation complex that meanders from indoors to outside and down a level or two for outdoor festivities the entire family can enjoy. The actual bathroom is located conveniently off the sun deck and includes a bath with shower and a board to sit on for getting the sand and mud off the feet. Peeking through the doorway is the inviting outdoor hot tub, commanding its own level high above the yard. Soft, colorful lounge chairs corner it for sunbathing or just an afternoon doze in the fresh air. From this height, the children's play area can be seen on the lower deck. A jungle gym set, a basketball hoop, a tricycle, are the traditional play items. But the real conversation piece is the old bathtub, now converted into a sandbox. On rainy days the wooden door lying beside it can be placed over this "sand tub" to keep the sand dry. Or when a workbench is required, the same door makes an indestructible tabletop. A strikingly clever use of porch and sun deck to accommodate the whole family—a family that can play, relax, and bathe in proximity and yet remain far enough from each other to preserve individuality and group harmony.

private bath tucked under the rafters when you convert your attic into a guest room. The ingenious adaptation of space can give what would be an ordinary bathroom a distinctive charm and character. The attic, the basement, the garage, a small alcove in the bedroom—if there is a need for a second bath or an additional half-bath, an unexpected bathing facility in an unexpected location will be a fascinating addition to your house.

*I*n order to enjoy a bathroom that goes beyond the bath, you must begin by thinking beyond the bath. The truly innovative bathrooms, for example, often separate into distinct areas the various functions that we have come to associate with the bathroom, dividing the bathroom into its original parts, as it were, giving each area its unique character by both decor and function. Historically, the activities of elimination, bathing, and dressing were considered separate and distinct. Even though a trend in recent years has been to include more and more of these personal activities in one large bathroom, such does not have to be the case. We can return to an earlier notion, that a tub can stand alone. An extra toilet is reason enough to transform a closet into a WC. Not every bathroom must have tub, shower, toilet, basin, and cabinetry.

Many rooms combining bed and bath already utilize this design concept. In a large, open bedroom, there might be sufficient room for a sunken or raised bathtub. A small bedroom can sometimes accommodate a basin and wash area. In either case, the unique attraction of a single bathroom

facility or fixture located in an unusual place gives the home that special distinctiveness, a boldness in concept, a willingness to defy convention.

The unusual space does not have to be outlandish. Sometimes it is developed by subduing a difficult space, taming an area that presents the designer with a seemingly impossible challenge. The room that is too narrow, too small, or inaccessible, when transformed into an entire bath or half-bath, can add a touch of the uncommon. An attic or basement area with a ceiling too low for most activities might become, with the necessary construction, an extra WC or a sunken bath or small shower. Even a room that seems inappropriate for a bathroom or that is considered too inconvenient for the family might become a sauna, a whirlpool, an additional toilet, or even a shaving station for the hectic morning rush hours.

It may seem like a step backward from civilized living, but consider the outbuildings and nearby storage sheds that with a major overhaul could be converted into mini bathing areas or entire bathrooms. Such a building, luxuriously furnished, well illuminated, and eminently private, across a garden or at the end of the patio, would in no way resemble the old, splintered shed with the crescent moon on the door to which our great-grandparents made midnight treks down the hill or out into the field.

*A*nother method of creating an unusual bathroom space, simple as it is, is the specialty or personalized bathroom: a private grooming or dressing area for the master or mistress of the

household, baths for the children segregated by sex or age, the guests' bathroom complete with luggage space.

When planning for a bathroom to be a special place in the home, the creative use of materials already present can frequently guarantee an unusual result. Overhead pipes do not have to be concealed, but they could be brightly painted. Old heaters can be equipped with towel racks so that they dry and warm towels or wet clothing hung near them. A fireplace and mantel should not be boarded up but fixed up, reflecting the theme of the bathroom and turning the hours spent there into truly romantic moments. Even a tree or fountain near the house could become, à la Frank Lloyd Wright, the centerpiece or corner support of a bathroom built onto the main building. Windows and skylights are obvious features that should be saved, not replaced. Views are as important in the bathroom as they are in the living room or bedroom. Light and ventilation are even more important.

*U*nusual spaces. They're everywhere if you but look for them. Look not only around the house but also in your imagination, because sometimes the most unusual, the most spectacular place must be created out of fantasies first. And if your home or apartment seems too small and ordinary for an unusual location, recall that "space" does not have to mean place or location. It can be mood, theme, feeling, experience. And sometimes all it takes is the one unusual feature, the one item of startling interest or appeal that can turn the ordinary bathroom into the extraordinary.

This bathing annex on the end of a modern suburban home epitomizes peace and relaxation. A sunken tub of pure white tile is trimmed with hand-painted blue and gold tiles in a room equally clean, pure, and neatly bordered by tile, plants, and windows. Natural light enters this room from several directions and levels—a skylight at the apex of the ceiling, sliding glass doors that open onto a small garden, and two long windows at staggered positions. One window illuminates the tub itself, offering the bather a restful view outdoors; the companion window higher up the wall completes the ensemble. This meticulously designed space is a small jewel of contemplative repose.

This wonderfully secluded outdoor place is
made entirely from natural materials that
blend right in to the wooded arbor that
protects it. This redwood hot tub can be
approached from several levels, and thus is
accessible to kids as well as adults. What
might have been long stairs running the
length of the deck were shortened to include
a wooden bench for sunning and drying off.
Notice the tubular shower stall, also
constructed from deck wood, just a few steps
from the hot tub, encouraging family and
guests to rinse off the dust and sweat of a
summer day before sliding into the relaxing
waters. A bright red punching bag, swing,
and overhead ladder for budding gymnasts
will complete an outdoor day of
sun, water, and exercise.

The good natured craziness of this bathroom-kitchen is seen in the Rousseau-like mural painted on the lower cabinet doors and the banana trees fanning the ceiling near the stove with their broad plumed leaves, bringing much imagined relief when the oven is on and the tub is steaming. Plastic goldfish dangle from the ceiling and real grapes and peaches pose on the table as a still life. Why all this madness in the first place? Because, as the owner expresses it, you can tend the supper simmering on the stove from a bubble bath, and should there be nothing cooking at the moment, there is always something interesting to look at or nibble on.

A mountain hideaway that makes no pretenses about the use of space—a bed, a tub, several trunks, and assortment of plants—this room sports a fine refuge of clutter to welcome home a person whose life is too engaged in the outdoors to be fussy about the necessities of bed and bath. And yet, this room has a comfortable lived-in quality to it that blends intention with happenstance, something more precious bed-and-bathrooms frequently lack. Here you can return from a strenuous hike or a mountain trek, doff boots and parka, and unwind with hot chocolate, a long soak, perhaps a peaceful nap. This room, like the mountains it faces, promises reliability. Like the challenging peaks in the distance, it will always be here, waiting for you.

This long, narrow room was not wide enough for a traditional rectangular bath, so a round tub was installed to treat the lack of space in the most efficient and satisfying fashion—a delightful "galley" bathroom. Splash tiles were extended up only the two walls to allow the much needed light to enter through the charming stained-glass window. By tiling only the galley walls at the far end, the designer has simulated extra depth in the room, suggesting a more spacious bathing area than really exists. A shower head directly above the tub is unobtrusive. When the shower curtain is removed (as shown here) this compact bathroom can seem almost double in size. Another subtle optical trick was to capitalize on the high ceiling by papering the walls with a thin vertical pattern, thus exploiting the one truly open feature of this room: height.

What would otherwise be a rather plain bathtub takes on a special grandeur when built into its own private alcove. Surrounded by an onyx wall and a dropped, arched ceiling, the tub turns this recess into a stately bathing area, brightened by light reflected in the mirror, which duplictes the clean, arched design of this bathing space. The unusual use of the mirror and the centrally located faucet and taps create the impression that this entire nook is really just a large basin and mirror—but a nook that invites the entire body to luxuriate while ensconced in an onyx cove away from the rest of the room.

The octagonal beams of this arboreal ceiling cover a most unusually constructed bathroom. The wood paneling of the interior moves outward to a bathing area of tile and brick open to the sky, plants, and a garden setting that is private and restful. The green vegetation as a motif is introduced into the interior foreground with the sensuously drooping branches that seem to grow right through the boundaries of the room. Notice the sparkle in the mosaic tiles that line the tub's interior. Washing in this bathroom is much like washing outdoors, in a curious space that is both open and closed, outside and inside at the same time.

When the kids grow up and leave home to start families of their own, the two- or three-car garage that was so indispensable during the adolescent years can be remodeled for other uses. For example, a guesthouse for visiting in-laws and grandchildren complete with its own bathroom. A simple tub installed where the kids used to store their bikes or jalopy will let you entertain your children's family without creating traffic jams in the master bathroom in the main house. The driveway can be converted into a patio for visiting. On nice days, the overhead door remains up for an open accessible space where grandchildren can run and play.

Mirrors can create unusual space even where there is no space. The bathroom above eerily appears to have two toilets, but on closer look we see that a mirror running at an angle from the potted orange bush by the toilet creates the illusion that there are two of everything. The optical deception is enhanced by the speckled effect of the wormy, spaghetti pattern on the wall tiles and the tight, crackled mosaic tiles on the floor. The relatively monotoned color of burnished gold and copper caps the viewer's puzzlement.

On the left is a bathroom built just off a bedroom of rather quiet, subdued colors. But pull back the drapes and a glittering surprise awaits you. The circular mosaic-tiled tub is reflected at least seven times in this cavern of mirrors. Almost no discernible corner is apparent as each mirror dissolves or multiplies actual wall surfaces.

Here is a bathroom-in-the-attic arrangement, utilizing a space limited by an extremely low ceiling. In fact, there is very little room to stand upright except in the very center. Working with and not against this major constraint, the washbasin has been built out into the center of the room and a slanted mirror installed along the dressing counter, where you can sit to brush your hair or apply cosmetics. The tub is tucked into the eaves at the far corner below the triangular window, which echoes the A-frame structure of the room. By using only wood and plaster, and leaving the bathroom free from extraneous decorations, the designer has capitalized on the beam-and-rafter motif—an honest bathroom reflecting the essence of its location in both materials and design.

There isn't much room up in the rafters of most homes, but a little ingenuity can transform the attic level into more than just a bedroom for guests or a rumpus room for kids. A private tub and shower come along with this remodeling design. Notice the raised floor, which conceals the added plumbing and elevates the bathroom facilities from the rest of the room. The floor is neatly tiled for waterproofing. A simple clear shower curtain provides the extra space for rinsing off standing up in this shallow, miniature tub. Stand up and spray down your soapy body with a quick shower—the tops of the trees just a few feet away from you outside the portico window offer substantial privacy. Not everyone gets the privilege of showering in an aviary!

7

Styles and Motifs

This Mediterranean-style bathroom is as bright as a Moroccan sun and as inviting as a deserted beach. Indeed, the accessories and knickknacks in the corner are clustered very much like shells, coral, sea wrack, and driftwood. The louvred shutters are typical of climates where the sun is intense and refreshing breezes are the only respite on a hot summer day. The bathing area is a molded unit that includes various levels surrounding the bathtub. A spectacular sea view from the window gives this bathroom a touch of reality—both inside and outside of this room the bather is in a romantic environment of sand, sea, and sun.

All bathrooms have style. Many of us grew up thinking there was no style for a bathroom, or that all bathrooms incorporated the same style: functional, modern, utilitarian. In fact, this style—uncomplicated and practical— was the dominant style of most bathrooms for many years in the middle of this century. But as the bathrooms displayed throughout this book attest, times change. And so does style.

What is style? A curious and elusive quality, like art itself. Basically it is a way of doing something, a mode of appearance, a recognizable type. The elements of style are indeed aesthetic and emotional factors: line, shape,

Promotional copy for this Victorian shower states: "The Bath is finished to stand without any woodwork or enclosure whatever. Only three joints are to make and the Bath is fixed, thus saving a large amount of carpenter and plumber work."

color, materials, form, texture, tone, and feeling. However limited by available techniques and materials, by the scope of one's imagination, style makes a statement.

This bath model patented by Shanks in the late nineteenth century won a prize medal at the Birmingham Health Exhibition. The soap and sponge tray is nickle-plated and the taps are advertised as "non-concussive quick-closing and quick-opening."

A wealth of bathing styles has developed over the centuries, embodying the tastes and values of other periods of history and other cultures.

Some early cultural groups, for instance, incorporated washing into religious rituals. The Hebrews washed away sin, the Hindus washed religiously at least three times a day, and the Muslims freshened up before praying. The Egyptians, realizing that the Nile was a divine gift, carefully channeled most of it into intricate irrigation systems needed for growing crops. Nevertheless, they bathed in the Nile, showered occasionally under water poured from pitchers (and then recycled into irrigation canals), and scented their bodies against the desert heat with sweet-smelling perfumes.

Of all the ancients, the Minoans on Crete enjoyed the most advanced bathing facilities. In King Minos's palace at Knossos, terra-cotta pipes lashed together with thongs through eyelets conducted running water indoors to a lavish assortment of baths, sinks, and even flush toilets. They were convenient, beautiful, and, for their day, the most hygienic bathing arrangements in the ancient world. Their nearby neighbors, the Greeks, were not

known for devoting so much time or trouble to bathing. Their sparsely furnished homes did not even include bathrooms. Having a street and marketplace culture, where front doors opened outward, the Greeks often limited their bathing to quick, cold showers following athletic and military events. Homer's "long-haired Greeks," therefore, were not the world's greatest shampooers.

The roads leading to Rome led to a city of enthusiastic bathers. The Eternal City could boast of bringing into the metropolis 300 gallons of water per person each day (more water than some major cities provide each citizen today) and, near the end of her glory,

This range of public urinals won a prize medal at the Congress of the Sanitary Institute, Newcastle, 1896. The design is a "cradle-back" slope rather than flat, a feature that "directs the urine and prevents sparking."

144 public latrines. These enormous quantities of water descended on the city through world-famous aqueducts, some of which are still standing, and

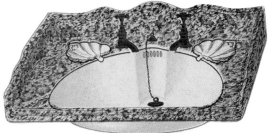

These new porcelain royal basins are advertised as "non-crazing" and are guaranteed to be so. Notice the recessed soap holders on each side of the bowl, the raised splash rims that create a boxlike effect for the entire lavatory, the delicate taps, and the stopper on a chain.

through lead pipes that purportedly killed off the upper classes with lead poisoning—an early example of advanced technology bringing its own health and environmental hazards.

Public baths in Rome were popular social and political centers, privy to the negotiations and discussions of senators, merchants, soldiers, shoppers, and prostitutes. Mall-like, the public baths, with their markets, libraries, museums, and sexual liaisons, attracted thousands of bathers every afternoon. For a bountiful "afternoon delight" a Roman enjoyed an oil rub, steam bath, swim, massage, skin scrape, and cold rinse. Outside the

cities, natural hot springs inspired health spas; and military bases usually had latrines consisting of multiholed seats lined up outhouse fashion over a running stream or the drainage canal from a bathhouse. Whether at home or on the road, the Romans sought to preserve their worthy ideal: *mens sana in corpore sano.*

As Christianity came to dominate the Western world there coincided a marked decline in bathing among the population as a whole. Whether because people considered the flesh to be weak and lavish bath rituals to be too self-indulgent for this "valley of tears," or because after the Crusades the Turkish influence of baths as opulent, sin-shaded oases was difficult to

This woodcut depicts the bathroom in the royal apartments in the Pitti Palace, Florence. These Renaissance rooms exuded the sumptuous and luxurious lifestyles of the upper class that was quickly aped by the rising middle classes in the prosperous Italian city-states.

reconcile with scholastic theology, less interest in physical hygiene was the order of the day. Except, ironically, among Christian monks whose daily order included warm baths, running water, separate taps, and ritual hand washing before meals. In fact, medieval monasteries kept alive the idea of the bath even as they tended the light of learning.

In England, that sceptered and septic isle, King John took a bath once every three weeks, and several centuries later Good Queen Bess bathed once a month, whether she needed it or not. The custom seemed to be about once every three to four weeks. In humbler homes bathing took place in a wooden tub shared by the entire family, to utilize the bath water while it was hot. Some castles had stone or

wooden toilet seats built into a shaft in the wall that led to a pit or sometimes to the moat itself, a fact that may have inspired the famous phrase "to wreak (reek?!) havoc on the enemy." In towns and villages, toilet habits were more hit and miss. Even if human ingenuity had devised a more sanitary procedure than urinating under the bed (dirt floors required!), in the fireplace, or along the wall outside, the lack of civic institutions to provide improved health services for everyone would have prevented it from becoming widespread. In fact, military needs might have stalled the developement of more healthful systems, since the urine-sodden soil was a source of the saltpeter used in explosives, and officials known as "petre-men" had authority to come in and dig up the uric crystals beneath one's bed. Folks on the second floor and those not fortunate enough to have dirt floors used a chamber pot, merrily emptied out the window to the warning "Gardy loo" (in England) or "Gardez l'eau" (in France); thus the modern expression of "Going to the loo," even though in the original one never had to actually *go* to it. It came to you.

The first real bathrooms, though, were usually converted bedrooms in large Victorian homes and resembled other rooms in the eclectic, overdecorated style of the late nineteeth century: ornate carpets, heavy drapes, massive furnishings, little light. Not until the turn of the century did bathrooms become stark, functional, antiseptically bare rooms designed for easy maintenance and quick visits. Styles and customs were changing, and even servents bathed at least once a week. The more affluent baths soon reflected Art Deco tastes, and flaunted glass, chrome, mirrors, and the cold, sleek two-toned look that boldly made peace with the modern world of industrial shapes and design.

By midcentury, bathtubs were coming equipped with showerheads and curtain rings, and, at least in America, the daily shower, the daily shampoo, and the daily use of deodorants (originally created only for people who "had a problem") were considered *de rigueur* for everyone. But no longer was only one style for the bath thought to be *de rigueur.*

Out of this long evolution of the bath came the many contemporary styles, patterns, and motifs of bath design. The simple country taste utilizes inexpensive, homemade items in an unpretentious and honest manner. The contemporary international style flaunts wealth and importance, an easy familiarity with the latest trends and novelties, a taste whose overall consistency in detail and theme suggests the talent of a professional designer. The Colonial style, from America's distant past, sports eighteenth-century furnishings, Queen Anne furniture, Chippendale cabinetry, ornately painted porcelain fixtures. A period closer to our own time, the Victorian, displayed baths that were plush with heavy, handsome furnishings that sought to express reliability, confidence, and middle class respectability.

Then there are the styles imported from more exotic regions. The Oriental style features minimal decoration, plain surfaces, and rectilinear geometry. The Mediterranean bath is characterized by a bright coolness in a sunny environment, where pastel colorings are interrupted by an occasional passionate flurry of deeper tones, and the rough, sandy surfaces of plaster and terra cotta are left naturally unadorned in a charmingly unfinished state. Tropical motifs can be created by dense foliage, irrepressible growth, brilliant colors, equatorial lavishness.

Some bath designs owe more to the contemporary scene than to history or regional culture. For example, minimalism strips the room of extraneous decor and equipment, creating bare, functional arrangements that are almost Oriental in their aesthetic use of empty space. Most recently, the funky style has caught on among people with a humorous sense of extravagance, a style that springs from the comic and the cartoonlike, a style excessively eclectic and outrageously daring in the

A circular stone tub discovered beneath the rotunda of a public bath at Pompeii. This building is typical of Rome's influence on the daily living habits of citizens throughout the empire. In large public baths commerce, politics, literature, and current events were discussed by citizens while they attended to the personal hygiene that was so crucial, since large numbers of people were clustered in urban environments.

playful misuse of pop objects. Migrating from loft apartments in converted warehouses to suburban homes, high tech boldly celebrates the steel, glass, and concrete world created by technological developments of the last half-century: exposed pipes, industrial colors and materials, commercial brands and models.

Lastly, many bathrooms, are designed specifically for sex or for the relationship between them. Traditionally masculine styles lean toward sturdy materials and hardy colors, a somewhat cluttered look that avoids the overly neat and excessive frills, decorative touches that are associated with male interests and pursuits. The feminine, on the other hand, has traditionally embodied a delicate, even pretty ambience, neatly arranged with vulnerable pastel colors and customary feminine objects such as flowers and perfumes. The romantic bathroom is seductive, sensuous, obviously designed for two, suggesting a warm privacy that invites dalliance and expressing the naughty tryst that excites the imagination toward thoughts of love and passion.

By selecting a style, you have chosen only the design frame of your bathroom, not the arrangement, the composition of parts. For example, not every Japanese-style bath looks the same. Not every country bathroom needs dried corn husks on the wall, nor must every feminine bathroom be pink. Within each style there is room for variations and personal preferences —a place to leave your signature. You can stamp the room with the character and values that are distinctively yours.

The bathrooms in this chapter are only a selection. Many others throughout this book could just as easily and justifiably have been included here. We selected these because they are especially distinctive, striking in style, bold in statement. Each is a product of a conscious effort to distinguish it by theme, style, type. Each possesses a unified, coherent look, motif, or mood that pervades the entire room.

We have also included a sampling of bathrooms, fixtures, and bathing customs from the past to honor the fundamental principle of all style: namely, style builds upon style. Even the creators of what seems to be an entirely new style learn, borrow, and adapt from those who have gone before them. Every new idea has a kernel of history embedded in it from an earlier period. Every new design concept is touched by the shadow of men and women whose influence extended beyond the immediate world in which they lived and created.

The beat and excitement of urban nightlife is expressed in this highly charged bathroom. A contemporary cavern of mirrors and stalactite light fixtures, this room produces an infinity of electric brilliance. A bouquet of pale yellow flowers graces the dark-marble basin, and a slender figure dances like a sprite with a hula hoop, both suggestive of the ephemeral quality of la dolce vita. *Here is a bathroom style that vibrates with the modern quest for thrills, spectacle, and glittering distraction. And yet as the blossoms and the slender dancer remind us, the fast-paced entertainment that characterizes much of contemporary life must make room for moments of balance and natural beauty.*

This bathroom furnished with Victorian fixtures painted bone white spotlights each piece of furniture against black walls and ceiling. A room of impeccable detail and grace, the stark black and the white contrasts suggest a harlequinesque balance. An ornate brocade trims the basin and Chippendale accessories rack above it. The beaded lamp shades and lace curtains epitomize the weightless delicacy that the designer intended for this room, all the more appreciated against the dark walls. In fact, each white object, be it tub, window frame, light fixture, or the old chain-pull flush tank, seems to float in a timelessness undisturbed by the mood or the season.

This very feminine bathroom is for the woman who is still very much a little girl at heart. Dainty peppermint pink netting touches every corner of this lovely room. The wicker chaise lounge, dressing stool, and rattan tables match the woven pattern of the pink and white fabric that is used so lavishly on walls, ceiling, cabinets, shelves, tub enclosure, and even the pillow coverings and curtain room divider. A room bright and ethereal, delicate as cotton candy. It is the kind of room that fills many little girls' fantasies at some point or other.

The safari style of this bathroom can almost be heard as well as seen—the shrill, piercing scream of jungle birds, the beat of drums, insects buzzing in the bush. The dense array of tropical plants and bamboo wall covering convey an entire world rather than the mere suggestion of a theme. Bathing in this setting and grooming before the mirror enveloped by thick jungle growth is an experience that thrusts the necessities of life—civilized or not—into the forefront of consciousness. How easy life among the "noble savages" on a South Sea isle must have been! How little effort was needed then to maintain that pure virginal freshness, the childlike innocence that the modern world has exiled from our lives.

This bathroom by Bonsack of London has a wonderfully unified look due to the simple color choice and the use of borders. The panels of the tub enclosure, the candy-cane trim on the tub's interior, even the drawers, curtains, lampshade, and cushioned stool employ the burgundy-beige combination of borders within borders. The process by which Bonsack creates each tub—many custom-designed for individual clients—safeguards all personal decorations, initials, monograms, and border designs. These distinctive tubs are light, easy to install, and, according to their designer, beautiful enough to allow the bathroom to become the "core of the house." And why not? People today seem to spend more and more waking hours in the bathroom.

The country look has returned to favor in recent years, especially in kitchens and bathrooms. Typical of country decor is the ample use of natural wood, seen here in window frame, cabinets, tub enclosure, and floor. The handmade rag rug lends a touch of rusticity to the simple floor, and the wooden-handled scrub brush sitting idly on the end of the tub harkens back to the pioneer days of quilting bees and corn-husking parties. Like simple farmfolk of a century ago, not yet linked electronically to the larger world of changing fashions, the owners of this humble bathroom have left it unadorned. There are almost no decorative touches that are not useful or homemade.

Here is a bathroom unabashedly direct in celebrating the high-tech look of the post-industrial world we live in. It playfully focuses on the pipes of many colors (coded by color as to function: hot, cold, electrical, heating, back flow, etc.). Metal beams and supports and the seemingly haphazard placement of fixtures convert this loft into a bright, airy bathing and dressing room. Shelves are completely open, clothing hangs on a rack in full view, protected by clear plastic coverings, and overhead storage areas are not concealed. What might appear to be a cold, empty warehouse is whimsically tempered by several lyrical touches: the rainbow of colors on pipes and heaters, the old-fashioned wooden dresser between the windows, and the idyllic rural view from the windows themselves. The result: pastoral high tech!

This very modern-looking bathroom is over fifty years old, but the designer was one of the forerunners of modern architecture. Created by Le Corbusier, in the Villa Savoye at Poissy, France, this starkly bare bathroom is a classic example of the influential Swiss architect's concept of the home as "a machine for living." The pure tile environment is a harbinger of the sleek, functional design of austere beauty. The contoured chaise lounge in the forefront has come back into fashion recently especially in the contoured plastic tubs that support the reclining body while bathing. The orange cubicle on the left is a display shelf, and the orange curtain rod across the top was used to screen the bath area from the rest of the bedroom, of which this bathroom is but one part.

This minimalist design shapes the clear lines and planes of the bath and shower area into a direct conceptual statement. The far wall panel with a window divides the shower from the rest of the room where a much larger window emits daylight. Because this wall does not reach to the ceiling, light can enter over the top and air can circulate unimpeded. The bath tiles are basic black and the walls are light, unsanded plaster, thus presenting a pleasing contrast in color and texture. Almost Mediterranean in its effect of simple decorum, this design successfully introduces the bathing area almost unannounced. Even the fixtures are understated. There are scarcely any extraneous objects.

Here is the type of minimalist bathroom our descendants may come to accept as traditional in a galaxy far away or on the spacecraft that carries them there. Modular panels, perfectly balanced, pointedly functional—the bare necessities of toilet, basin, mirror, and shower. An antiseptically clean room, stripped of all expressionistic individuality and extraneous decor. The mathematical precision in this design achieves a pleasing sterility. Unencumbered by art or culture, undistracted by a sense of time or place, this bathroom means business—a place one does not tarry or linger in while there is so much universe yet to explore.

This serene, minimalist room invites you to lounge around the tub as much as it seduces you into the water. No cold floors under bare feet for these bathers! In fact, the sensuous carpeting might even tempt you and a friend to stretch out on it after a bath and let its soft caressing fibers dry your skin by soaking up the water naturally. The black walls set off the white circular tub that dominates this room while the three levels seem to fold rather than step up to it. Two plain white towels are all that is needed to highlight the dark wall. A room devoid of color, where texture says it all, and desire says even more!

In a word—elegance. In this bathroom, luxury and good taste prevail.
The marbled effect of floor, tub enclosure, and resting slab
contains a rich green grain that tinges the entire room with a
subdued quiet and repose. Striking orange birds-of-paradise stand as
tall sentinels at each end of this substantial tub. An expansive mirror
over the tub creates an alluring depth of darkness and mystery. In a
room so serenely appointed and perfectly controlled, the brilliant red
lacquered chair and the supply of sensuous gold-corded green towels
await in a mood of splendid seduction. A bather here can feel the lure,
the spell that curiously blends elegance and eroticism in an
atmosphere imposingly sumptuous.

Sources/
Useful Addresses

UNITED STATES

Fixtures: baths, toilets, etc.

AART CULTURED MARBLE
1325 Egbert Avenue
San Francisco, CA 94124
(415) 822-9555

AMERICAN BIDET
P.O. Box 1500
Hollywood, FL 33022
(305) 922-2222

AMERICAN STANDARD
P.O. Box 2003
New Brunswick, NJ 08903
(201) 885-1900

BATHS INTERNATIONAL
89 Fifth Avenue
New York, NY 10003
(212) 242-7158

CHRISTINA UNLIMITED OF CALIFORNIA
320 Fell Street
San Francisco, CA 94102
(415) 431-0066

DAVIS AND WARSHOW
150 East 58th Street
New York, NY 10022
(212) 987-0966

ELJER PLUMBINGWARE
Three Gateway Center
Pittsburgh, PA 15222
(412) 553-7200

HASTINGS IL BAGNO
201 East 57th Street
New York, NY 10022
(212) 755-2710

JENNINGS SALVAGE
1523 San Pablo Avenue
Berkeley, CA 94702
(415) 526-1008

KIMSTOCK SOUTHWEST
913 North Main Street
Hutchins, TX 75141
(214) 527-1876

MARBLE FACTORY
15168 Raymer
Van Nuys, CA 94124
(213) 988-4467

MAR-DECO MANUFACTURERS
1350 Egbert Avenue
San Francisco, CA 94124
(415) 822-3244

PENN PIPE AND SUPPLY
1121 Dale Avenue
Seanton, CA 90680
(415) 585-7366

RAIN JET CORPORATION
27671 La Paz Road
Laguna Niguel, CA 92677
(714) 643-0444

SHERLE WAGNER
60 West 57th Street
New York, NY 10022
(212) 758-3300

SASSUOLO CERAMIC IMPORTS
2809 Gough Street
San Francisco, CA 94123
(415) 928-1677

SUNRISE SALVAGE
2210 San Pablo Avenue
Berkeley, CA 94702
(415) 229-4702

SYN-MAR CULTURED MARBLE
220 Bayshore Boulevard
San Francisco, CA 94124
(415) 285-5995

THE TILE SHOP
1005 Harrison Street
Berkeley, CA 94710
(415) 525-4312

Accessories: fittings, linens, towels, etc.

BATH AND BOUDOIR SHOP
900 North Point
Ghiradelli Square
San Francisco, CA 94109
(415) 474-7282

BATH BAZAAR
1130 Polk Street
San Francisco, CA 94109
(415) 567-9639

BATH BOUTIQUE
2076 Chestnut Street
San Francisco, CA 94123
(415) 567-9636

BATHROOM JEWELRY
1888 South Sepulveda Boulevard
West Los Angeles, CA 90049
(213) 478-0237

BEYLERIAN
305 East 63rd Street
New York, NY 10021
(212) 755-6303

ELEGANT JOHN OF LEXINGTON AVENUE
812 Lexington Avenue
New York, NY 10021
(212) 935-5800

THE FINAL TOUCH BATH AND CLOSET
BOUTIQUE
18217 Dixie Highway
Homewood, IL 60430
(312) 798-6433

HORTON AND CONVERSE
11600 Wilshire Boulevard
Brentwood, CA 90025
(213) 478-0810

J. ABOUCHAR AND SONS
104 West 40th Street
New York, NY 10018
(212) 840-0602

JANOVIC PLAZA
Third Avenue at 67th Street
New York, NY 10021
(212) 243-2186

LENNY'S LINEN CLOSET
1851 Union Street
San Francisco, CA 94123
(415) 931-1424

LINEN WORLD
5225 South Harper Avenue
Chicago, IL 60615
(312) 955-0100

LINENS PLUS
2801 South Robertson Boulevard
Los Angeles CA 90034
(213) 204-1181

MINKA'S BATH AND LINENS
325 Beverly Drive
Beverly Hills, CA 90210
(213) 275-8885

MIRROR MIRROR BATH SHOP
67 Serramonte Center
Daily City, CA 94105
(415) 994-5987

ROYAL FLUSH BATH SHOP
1122 Lake Street
Oak Park, IL 60301
(312) 383-2940

TILE CENTER INCORPORATED
1041 Madison Street
Oak Park, IL 60302
(312) 287-2940

TOUCH OF ELEGANCE BY CARMEL
1163 Wilmette Avenue
Wilmette, IL 60091
(312) 256-4220

WESTWOOD BATH BOUTIQUE
10583 West Pico Boulevard
Los Angeles, CA 90064
(213) 475-6185

Lighting
THE APARTMENT DWELLER
604 Second Avenue
New York, NY 10016
(212) 532-1706

BRENTWOOD LIGHTING COMPANY
11961 South Vincente Boulevard
Los Angeles, CA 94901
(213) 472-6575

COLLIER LIGHTING INCORPORATED
1595 Frisco Boulevard
San Rafael, CA 94901
(415) 454-6672

DRAMATIC LIGHTING EFFECTS
346 West 44th Street
New York, NY 10036
(212) 489-1370

ELEGANT LIGHTING
1550 Westwood Boulevard
Los Angeles, CA 90024
(213) 475-4548

FANTASY LITES
7126 Melrose Avenue
West Hollywood, CA 90024
(213) 933-7244

THE FELDMAN COMPANY
853 North La Cienega Boulevard
Los Angeles, CA 90069
(213) 652-1488

GEKEE FIBEROPTICS
P.O. Box 5771
Stanford, CA 94303
(415) 494-1350

LEE MARLENE LIGHTING DESIGN
CONSULTING ENGINEERS
573 Mission Street
San Francisco, CA 94105
(415) 546-7885

LEE'S STUDIO GALLERY
211 West 57th Street
New York, NY 10019
(212) 265-5670

LET THERE BE NEON
451 West Broadway
New York, NY 10012
(212) 473-7370

LUMINAE LIGHTING CONSULTANTS
2015 17th Street
San Francisco, CA 94103
(415) 552-1010

NEON NEON
3692 17th Street
San Francisco, CA 94116
(415) 552-4163

NEUMANN METAL STUDIO
741 Clementia
San Francisco, CA 94103
(415) 552-7678

NEW RENAISSANCE GLASS WORKS
5151 Broadway
Oakland, CA 94611
(415) 653-1231

PHOENIX DAY COMPANY
51 Washburn
San Francisco, CA 94103
(415) 863-6655

SOLUX CORPORATION
58-17 28th Avenue
Woodside, NY 11377
(212) 726-1300

STURCTURA
171 Bowery
New York, NY 10002
(212) 966-0757

TURPAN SANDERS
386 West Broadway
New York, NY 10012
(212) 925-9040

Custom Design and Renovation
A. A. HOKOM CORPORATION
400 North Beverly Drive
Beverly Hills, CA 90210
(213) 275-4121

A BANK STREET CARPENTER
2 Bank Street
New York, NY 10014
(212) 675-2381

ABC PAVILLION INCORPORATED
45 West 34th Street
New York, NY 10001
(212) 868-1011

BATH AND SPA DESIGN SHOWCASE
541 8th Street
San Francisco, CA 94118
(415) 626-7400

THE BATH WORKS
Route 22 and West End Avenue
North Plainfield, NJ 07061
(201) 757-3232

CARACALLA
969 Third Avenue
New York, NY 10022
(212) 753-9322

DEL MONT BUILDERS
2142 West 95th Street
Chicago, IL 60643
(312) 881-4900

FRED ALLEN DESIGN ASSOCIATES
677 Fifth Avenue
New York, NY 10019
(212) 308-0831

JAN'S BATHROOMS AND KITCHENS
1065 West Madison Street
Chicago, IL 60607
(312) 226-2432

LUSTY MODULAR SYSTEMS
8910 Beverly Boulevard
Los Angeles, CA 90048
(213) 550-0648

SMOLKA
182 Madison Avenue
New York, NY 10016
(212) 879-1200

Storage

ABSTRACTA STRUCTURES
101 Park Avenue
New York, NY 10017
(212) 944-2244

AMERICAN HOME ACCESSORIES
686 Lexington Avenue
New York, NY 10022
(212) 688-6568

CLOSET KING
458 Greenwich Street
New York, NY 10013
(212) 734-2178

CORSICAN FURNITURE
2437 East 24th Street
Los Angeles, CA 90058
(213) 587-3101

DELCORT WALL SYSTEMS PLUS
1017 Clement Street
San Francisco, CA 94118
(415) 668-6066

DESIGN DYNAMICS
1032 Clement Street
San Francisco, CA 94118
(415) 668-4131

ELEGANT WICKER AND WOOD
1233 Sutter Street
San Francisco, CA 94109
(415) 673-7831

KING CUSTOM VANITIES
5158 Woodley Avenue
Encino, CA 91316
(213) 789-2856

MARBLE CRAFT
6567 North Olmstead
Chicago, IL 60631
(312) 763-3790

NEW DIMENSIONS
3020 Polk Street
San Francisco, CA 94109
(415) 928-5967

PETER PEPPER PRODUCTS
17929 South Susana Road
Compton, CA 90221
(213) 979-0815

RUTT CUSTOM WOOD
1086 East Gun Hill Road
Bronx, NY 10469
(212) 547-1600

TECHNIQUES IN WOOD
P.O. Box 594
8 Carin Street
Rochester, NY 14602
(716) 328-3800

VAN GEMERT DESIGN CABINETRY
7101 West Addison Street
Chicago, IL 60634
(312) 777-9131

VIRCO MANUFACTURING CORPORATION
P.O. Box 44846
Hancock Station
Los Angeles, CA 90044
(213) 321-3400

Toiletries, cosmetics, oils, etc.

BARE ESSENTIALS
317 Connecticut Street
San Francisco, CA 94107
(415) 641-0750

THE BATH HOUSE
215 Thompson Street
New York, NY 10013
(212) 533-0690

BOYD CHEMISTS
655 Madison Avenue
New York, NY 10021
(212) 838-6558

CASWELL-MASSEY
Lexington Avenue at 48th Street
New York, NY 10017
(212) 755-2257

ESSENTIAL PRODUCTS COMPANY
90 Water Street
New York, NY 10005
(212) 344-4288

HANKY PANKY
3315 Sacramento Avenue
San Francisco, CA 94118
(415) 346-4791

OCEANS OF LOTIONS
1545 Clement Road
San Francisco CA 94118
(415) 221-3747

THE PERFECT SCENT
1797 Market Street
San Francisco, CA 94103
(415) 626-3810

SKIN ZONE
531 Castro Street
San Francisco, CA 94118
(415) 626-7933

TUB AND SCRUB BATHIQUE
64 Westlake Mall
San Francisco, CA 94105
(415) 755-3938

VILLAGE BATH PRODUCTS
Box 1A
Minnetonka, MN 55343
(612) 328-5928

ZITOMER PHARMACY
998 Madison Avenue
New York, NY 10021
(212) 737-4480

Jacuzzis, Hot Tubs, Saunas

BATHS INTERNATIONAL
89 Fifth Avenue
New York, NY 10003
(212) 242-7158

CALIFORNIA HOT TUBS
60 Third Avenue
New York, NY 10003
(212) 982-3000

CECIL ELLIS SAUNA AND LEISURE
CORPORATION
99 White Birch Road
New Canaan, CT 06840
(800) 243-6764

DAN LURI SAUNA CORPORATION
1671 Utica Avenue
Brooklyn, NY 11234
(212) 258-3900

GORDON AND GRANT
423 North Quarantina
Santa Barbara, CA 92109
(805) 963-5353

JACUZZI ® WHIRLPOOL BATH COMPANY
1129 Bloomfield Avenue
West Caldwell, NJ 07006
(201) 575-7710

JACUZZI ® WHIRLPOOL BATH COMPANY
298 NORTH WIGET LANE
Walnut Creek, CA 94596
(415) 938-7070

MacLEVY PRODUCTS
43-23 91st Place
Elmhurst, NY 11373
(800) 221-0227

SAN DIEGO HOT TUBS
960 Grand Avenue
San Diego, CA 92109
(619) 483-3320

VIKING SAUNA COMPANY
P.O. Box 76121
Atlanta, GA 30328
(800) 538-7564

Floors and Walls (tile, stone, fabric, windows, blinds, etc.)

AMSTERDAM CORPORATION
950 Third Avenue
New York, NY 10022
(212) 644-1350

ANNICK'S STUDIO
422 Ramona Street
Palo Alto, CA 94301
(415) 327-6063

ARIE'S WALL UPHOLSTERERS
5140 Colfax Avenue
North Hollywood, CA 91601
(213) 769-0262

ART AND SOUL
24772 Mulholland Highways
Calabasas, CA 91302
(213) 716-0999

CANOVA MARBLE INCORPORATED
5835 Hollis Street
Emeryville, CA 94608
(415) 653-1809

CARRARA MARBLE AND MOSAICS
2202 North Natchez Avenue
Chicago, IL 60635
(312) 237-0415

CHIC TILE
1180 El Camino Real
Belmont, CA 94002
(415) 591-0318

COLOR SCHEME
2047 Fillmore
San Francisco, CA 94115
(415) 346-0700

CREATIVE PAINT AND WALL PAPER
999 Geary
San Francisco, CA 94109
(415) 441-8850

CROCE AND MONDELL COMPANY
2139 North Harlem Avenue
Chicago, IL 60635
(312) 237-6359

DECORET WALL SYSTEMS PLUS
1017 Clement Street
San Francisco, CA 94118
(415) 668-6066

DESIGN DYNAMICS
1032 Clement Street
San Francisco, CA 94118
(415) 668-4131

DUNN-EDWARDS PAINT
2201 Junipero Serra Boulevard
Daily City, CA 94015
(415) 992-9660

ENVIRONMENTAL GRAPHICS
622 Clement Street
San Francisco, CA 94118
(415) 751-6000

FORO MARBLE
566 President Street
Brooklyn, NY 11215
(212) 852-2322

HAMAR BROTHERS TILE
1290 Powell Street
Emeryville, CA 94608
(415) 658-7535

HASTINGS TILE COMPANY
201 East 57th Street
New York, NY 10022
(212) 755-2701

IMPORT TILE COMPANY
611 Hearst Avenue
Berkeley, CA 94701
(415) 843-5744

INNOVATIVE TILE AND SUPPLY
1850 Sawtelle Boulevard
Los Angeles, CA 90025
(213) 478-2506

ITALIAN TERRAZZO MAINTENANCE
INCORPORATED
612 North Sepulveda Boulevard
Los Angeles, CA 90049
(213) 472-9896

L. A. PAINT AND PAPER
7985 Santa Monica Boulevard
Los Angeles, CA 90046
(213) 656-0258

THE MASON'S ART
P.O. Box 301
Ross, CA 94957
(415) 459-0605

NEW YORK MARBLE
1399 Park Avenue
New York, NY 10029
(212) 534-2242

PLAIN AND FANCY TILE
714 East Green Street
Pasadena, CA 91101
(213) 577-2830

SEARS, ROEBUCK AND COMPANY
Sears Towers
Chicago, IL 60684
(312) 875-2500

TILE OUTLET
2434 West Fullerton
Chicago, IL 60642
(312) 276-2660

THE TILE SHOP
1005 Harrison Street
Berkeley, CA 94710
(415) 525-4312

TILE SHOWROOM
15020 Keswick Street
Van Nuys, CA 91405
(213) 787-7310

TILE WORKS
6265 North Sepulveda Boulevard
Van Nuys, CA 91411
(213) 786-8453

TILE WORLD
7901 Garden Grove Boulevard
Garden Grove, CA 92641
(714) 891-5935

VENETIAN NATURAL MARBLE COMPANY
991 Harrison Street
San Francisco, CA 94107
(415) 392-6379

W. F. JOHNSON COMPANY
8202 West 3rd Street
Los Angeles, CA 90048
(213) 653-1054

THE WALLPAPER FAIR
12400 Santa Monica Boulevard
West Los Angeles, CA 90025
(213) 820-2649

WESTERN STATES STONE COMPANY
30132 Industrial Parkway
Hayward, CA 94544
(415) 471-0755

UNITED KINGDOM

Fixtures

A BIGGER SPLASH
119 Fulham Road
London SW3
(01) 504-7454

ARMITAGE SHANKS LTD
Armitage
Rugeley
Staffordshire WS15 4BT
0543-490253

BATHROOM IDEAS
Bathroom Advisory Service
44 Earlham Street
London WC2
(01) 240-0959

BATHROOM & SHOWER CENTRE
204 Great Portland Street
London W1N 6AT
(01) 388-7631

BATHROOMS PLUS
19 Kensington Court Place
London W8
(01) 937-5858

BONSACK BATHS (LONDON) LTD
14 Mount Street
London W1Y 5RA
(01) 629-9981

B & P WYNN & CO
Crosshold House
18 Boston Parade
London W7 2DG
(01) 567-8758

C P HART
Newnham Terrace
Hercules Road
London SE1
(01) 928-5866

CZECH & SPEAKE
39c Jermyn Street
London SW1
(01) 980-1106

EWINGS
98 Cheetham Hill Road
Manchester M4 4EG
(061) 832-2309

FORMA, VICTOR R MANN & CO LTD
Unit 3
Mitcham Industrial Estate
85 Streatham Road
Mitcham
Surrey CR4 2AP
(01) 640-6811

GALLERIA MONTE CARLO
66-67 South Audley Street
London W1
(01) 493-6481

IDEAL STANDARD LTD
PO Box 60
National Avenue
Hull HU5 4JE
0482-499597

ROYAL DOULTON
Whieldon Road
Stoke-on-Trent ST4 4HN
0782-49191

S POLLIAK LTD
Norton
Malton
North Yorkshire Y017 9SQ
0653-5331

S.D.S. LUXURY BATHROOMS
179-189 Northcote Road
London SW11 6QF
(01) 228-1184

SITTING PRETTY
131 Devies Road
London SW6

ST. MARCO'S BATHROOMS
45 Soan Street
London W1
(01) 235-4833

TWYFORDS LTD
PO Box 23
Stoke-on-Trent ST4 7AL
0782-29531

WEST ONE BATHROOMS
18 North Audley Street
London W1
(01) 499-1845

Custom Design/ All-in-one Shop (Hot Tubs/Jacuzzis/Saunas)

FINNISH SAUNA BATHS
4 Shelbourne Close
Pinner, Middlesex
(01) 868-7170

INTERSCAN LEISURE PRODUCTS
Balmoral Road
Gillingham, Kent
0634-576851

JACUZZI WHIRLPOOL BATH CENTRE
157 Sloane Street
London SW1
(01) 730-5835

KOTISAUNA
Angel Drove
Ely, Cambridgeshire
0353-5764

MAX PIKE'S WHIRLPOOL BATH CENTRE
Unit 5/4 Eccleston Street
London SW1
(01) 730-7216

WHIRLPOOL BATH SYSTEMS
350 Fulham Road
London SW10
(01) 352-5794

Accessories: Fittings, Linens, Towels, etc.

BETWEEN THE SHEETS
190 Kensington Park Road
London W11
(01) 727-8768

EN SUITE
56 Cavendish Street
London W1
(01) 486-4140

HABITAT DESIGNS (HEAD OFFICE)
Hithercroft Road
Wallingford, Berkshire
0491-35511

HABITAT DESIGNS
156 Tottenham Court Road
London W1
(01) 387-9021

Lighting

LIGHTING ARTISTS
Hillview, Vale of Health
London NW3
(01) 431-2345

LIGHTING DESIGN SERVICE
205 Kentish Town Road
London NW5
(01) 267-9391

LONDON LIGHTING COMPANY
37 George Street
London W1
(01) 486-8825

Walls & Floors

DEEJAY FLOORING
1593 London Road
London SW16
(01) 679-1063

PLUSH FLUSH
27 Sackville Street
London W1
(01) 439-4315

Toiletries, etc.

BODYWISE
250 King's Road
London SW3
(01) 351-5688

THE BODY SHOP
22 Cheapside
London EC2
(01) 248-3410

CANADA

Fixtures

AMERICAN STANDARD:
1111 Finch Avenue West
Suite 101
Downsview, Ont.
M3J 2E5 (416) 665-8222

655 rue Hodge
Ville Sainte Laurent
Montreal, Canada
H4N 2A3 (514)747-7513

6450 Roberts Street
Burnaby, B.C.
V5G 4E1 (604)299-8801

10460 Mayfield Road
Unit #1100
Edmonton, Alberta
T5P 4P4 (403)483-8352

3220-5th Avenue North East
Calgary, Alberta
T2A 5N1

217-530 Century Street
Winnipeg, Manitoba
R3H 0Y4 (204)774-2466

BEST PLUMBING
11703-154th Street
Edmonton, Alberta
T5M 3X9 (403)451-2432

CANA-RONA
2673 Steeles Avenue West
Downsview, Ont.
M3J 2Z8 (416)661-8679

IDEAL
340 Lynn Avenue
North Vancouver, B.C.
V7J 2C5 (604)980-3467

SALRO
976 Montcon Avenue
Quebec City, P.Q.

SCHOCK COLLECTION
466 Trafalger Road
Oakville, Ont.

Accessories: Linens, Shower curtains, etc.

JAMES B. MC GREGOR MANUFACTURERS
103-249-½ Notre Dame Avenue
Winnipeg, Manitoba
R3B 1N8 (204)947-0750

UNIQUE BATH BOUTIQUE
2080-4th Avenue
Vancouver, B.C.
V6J 1M9 (604)733-3226

Lighting

THE OLD LAMP SHOP
1582 Queen Street East
Toronto, Ont.

Walls & Floors

AGINCOURT INTERIORS
4155 Sheppard Avenue East
Toronto, Ont.
M1S 1T4 (416)293-6641

ALLEEN'S WINDOW AND WALL
COVERINGS
444 Yonge Street
Unit C44
Toronto, Ont.
M5B 2H4 (416)977-2551

THE CEILING CENTER LIMITED
5070 Dundas Street West
Toronto, Ont.
M9A 1B9 (416)239-9201

DREAM DECOR LIMITED
4271 Sheppard Avenue East
Toronto, Ont.
M1S 4G4 (416)222-9834

THE GREAT COVER UP
687 Mount Pleasant Road
Toronto, Ont.
M4S 2N2 (416)485-4102

MacFLEMMING PAINT & WALLPAPER
5171 Yonge Street
Toronto, Ont.

SUNWORTHY WALLCOVERINGS
195 Walker Drive
Brampton, Ont.
L6T 3Z9

VAST INTERIORS
6 Cranbrooke Avenue
Toronto, Ont.
M5M 1M4 (416)488-2473

Storage

DWIGHT TAFFE DESIGNS
312 Seaton Street
Toronto, Ont.
M5A 2T7
(416)368-9534 or 924-8550

Custom Design/ All-in-one Shop

A WAY OF LIVING PRODUCTS
11200 River Road
Richmond, B.C.
V6X 1Z5 (604)278-3888

BATHROOMS BEAUTIFUL
Oakridge Shopping Center
#146-650 West 41st Street
Vancouver, B.C.
V5Z 2M9 (604)266-8811

BATHROOMS BEAUTIFUL
843 North Park Royal
West Vancouver, B.C.
V7T 1H9 (604)926-5122

CERAMIC DECOR ONTARIO LIMITED
4544 Dufferin Street
Toronto, Ont.
M3H 5X2 (416)665-8787

CERAMIQUE DECOR
4220 3eme Avenue
Quest, Quebec, PQ
G1H 6T1 (418)627-0122

FLOYD AND GERRARD LANDSCAPE
ARCHITECTS
289 Lisgar Street
Toronto, Ont.
M6J 3H1 (416)536-1617

GINGER'S BATHROOMS
945 Eglinton Avenue East
Toronto, Ont.
M4G 4B5 (416)429-3444

THE JOHN WHOLESALE
4700 Dufferin Street
Toronto, Ont.
M3H 5S7 (416)665-5980

NEIL TURNBULL LIMITED
24 Juniper Avenue
Toronto Ont.
M4L 1S3 (416)691-0443

ROBERTSON WATERWORKS
166 Sherbrook Street
Winnipeg, Manitoba
R3C 2B6 (204)772-2404

DANS UN JARDIN
Renaissance Plaza
150 Bloor Street West
Toronto, Ont.
M5S 2X9
(416)921-5119

ITALY

CESAME
Zona Industriale 2ª Stada
95100 Catania
Tel: 095 591 044

F.LLI FANTINI SpA
Via Buonarroti 4
280 10 Pella (NO)
Tel: 0322 969 127

IDEAL STANDARD
Via Ampere 102
20131 Milan
Tel: 02 2888

JACUZZI EUROPE SpA
S.S. Pontebbana km 97,200
33098 Valvasone (PN)
Tel: 0434 85 141

NOVELLO SpA
Divisione Arredament per Bagno
30035 Mirano (VE)
Italy CP 76
Tel: 041 430 733

RASPEL SpA
Via Volta 13
20019 Settimo Milanese
Tel: 02 328 5851

RUBINETTERIE STELLA SpA
Via Unita d'Italia 1
28100 Novara
Tel: 0321 473 351

RUBINETTERIE ZAZZERI SaS
Via di Rosana
Loc. Vallina
50012 Bagno a Ripoli
Florence
Tel: 055 691 051

TEUCO GUZZINI SrL
Via Passionisti 40
62019 Recanati (Macerata)
Tel: 071 981 444

FRANCE

BATHROOM GRAFFITI
22 rue Madeleine-Michelis
92 Neuilly-sur-Seine
Tel: (1)-745-8525

JACOB DELAFON
8 Place d'Iéna
75783 Paris, Cedex 16
Tel: (1)-505 13 37

J DELEPINE SA
104 Boulevard de Clichy
75108 Paris
Tel: (1)-606 89 70

FRANCÉMAIL
13 Boulevard Maleherbes
75008 Paris
Tel: (1)-265 63 65

FRANKE-FRANCE
ave A.-Briand
60230 Chambly BP 13
TEl: (3)-034 93 60

IDEAL STANDARD
149 Boulevard Haussmann
75008 Paris
Tel: (1)-563 01 80

PORCHER
75-77 Boulevard Victor-Hugo
93404 St Ouen
Tel: (1)-257 11 55

SCELLIER GAUTHIER
140 ave Ledru Rollin
75011 Paris
Tel: (1)-379 53 20

GERMANY

HEWI H WILKE GmbH
PO Box 1266
3548 Arolsen
Tel: 05691 82 1

E HOESCH & SÖHNE KUNSTOFFWERK KG
PO Box 550
51600 Düren
West Germany
Tel: 2421 61052

HÜPPA SANITÄRTECHNIK GmbH & CO KG
PO Box 2521
Stau 87-91
D-2900 Oldenburg
Tel: 04 41 2 42 55

IDEAL STANDARD GmbH
PO Box 1809
5300 Bonn 1
Tel: 01049 228 5211

KLAFS SAUNABAU GmbH & CO
Klafs-Strasse 179/2
7170 Schwäbisch Hall
Tel: 0791/50 10

LAUFEN
AG für Keramische Industrie
CH-4242 Laufen
Tel: 061 89 1011

PAUSER GmbH & CO KG
7075 Mutlangen
Tel: 07171 78 11

SAUNALUX GmbH
Hauptstrasse 10-18
D-6424 Grebenhain 4
Tel: 066 44 7061

VILLERY & BOCH
PO Box 120
6642 Mettlach
Tel: 01049 6864811

PICTURE CREDITS

A Bigger Splash *40 (right), 51 (both photos)*
Abitare/Silvio Wolf *113 (both photos)*
Bonsack Baths (London) Ltd. *112 (left)*
Karen Busolini *101*
Consulat *38 (left)*
Czech & Speake Ltd. *38 (right), 48, 49 (both photos), 50, 53 (left)*
John Donat *39 (right), 114*
EWA *41 (right), 54 (left)*
EWA/Michael Crockett *40 (bottom)*
EWA/Clive Helm *35 (left), 63*
EWA/Ann Kelly *12 (left)*
EWA/Neil Lorimer *4 (upper left), 12 (right), 21, 32, 34, 42 (right), 44, 70, 75, 88, 96 (left), 99 (right)*
EWA/Grant Mudford *110*
EWA/Michael Nicholson *15, 20 (right), 22 (both photos), 54 (right), 64 (right), 74, 76, 96 (right), 109 (both photos), 116, 117*
EWA/Julian Nieman *99 (left)*
EWA/Spike Powell *79*
EWA/Tim Street–Porter *4 (lower right), 11, 18, 26, 31 (both photos), 36, 42 (left), 47, 56, 58, 67 (both photos), 77, 80, 82, 83, 98, 115*
EWA/Jerry Tubby *20 (left), 111 (both photos)*

Forma/Victor R. Mann & Co., Ltd. *35 (right), 40 (top)*
Angelo Hornack *104 (all photos), 105 (left)*
Constance Leslie *13 (upper and lower right)*
Norman McGrath *6, 17 (left), 19, 27, 78, 84 (left), 93, 97*
Peter Paige *9 (interior design by Rona Levine), 37, 41 (left), 65 (interior design by HQZ Enterprises), 66 (interior design by EL Design), 86, 118 (interior design by Antine/Polo)*
Robert Perron *23, 24*
Royal Doulton *14*
Schöner Wohnen *55 (both photos)*
Sherle Wagner *108*
Liesa Siegelmann *64 (left), 84 (right), 85*
Siesel/Reni Kuhn *25, 59, 73, 87*
The World Of Interiors/James Mortimer *69, 102*
The World Of Interiors/Arabella McNair Wilson *95 (left)*
Jerry Tubby *13 (upper left)*
Twyfords Bathrooms *16*
Jeffrey Weiss *17 (right), 43, 52, 53 (right), 60, 61, 62, 68, 81, 90 (both photos), 91, 94, 95 (right), 100, 112 (right)*
Zazzeri Rubinetterie *39 (left)*

Cover photo by Peter Paige
Interior design by Antine/Polo